C000285046

GLOBAL ASSET ALLOCATION

A SURVEY OF THE WORLD'S TOP INVESTMENT STRATEGIES

MEB FABER

COPYRIGHT © 2015 THE IDEA FARM, LP

All rights reserved.

Limit of Liability/Disclaimer of Warranty: While the publisher and the author have used their best efforts in preparing this book, they make no representations or warranties with respect to the accuracy or completeness of the contents of this book and specially disclaim any implied warranties of merchantability or fitness for a particular purpose. No warranty may be created or extended by sales representatives or written sales materials. The advice and strategies contained herein may not be suitable for your situation. You should consult with a professional where appropriate. Neither the publisher nor author shall be liable for any loss of profit or any other commercial damages, including but not limited to special, incidental, consequential, or other damages. No part of this publication may be reproduced, stored in a retrieval system, or transmitted in any form or by any means, electronic, mechanical, photocopying, recording, scanning, or otherwise, except as permitted under Section 107 or 108 of the 1976 Unites States Copyright Act, without either the prior written permission of the Publisher, or authorization through payment of the appropriate per copy fee.

GLOBAL ASSET ALLOCATION

A Survey of the World's Top Investment Strategies

ISBN 978-0-9886799-2-4

FIRST EDITION

to Mom

ABOUT THE AUTHOR

Mr. Faber is a co-founder and the Chief Investment Officer of Cambria Investment Management, LP. Faber is the manager of Cambria's ETFs, separate accounts, and private investment funds for accredited investors. Mr. Faber is also the author of the Meb Faber Research blog, *Shareholder Yield*, *Global Value*, and the co-author of *The Ivy Portfolio: How to Invest Like the Top Endowments and Avoid Bear Markets*. He is a frequent speaker and writer on investment strategies and has been featured in *Barron's*, *The New York Times*, and *The New Yorker*. Mr. Faber graduated from the University of Virginia with degrees in Engineering Science and Biology. He is a Chartered Alternative Investment Analyst (CAIA), and Chartered Market Technician (CMT).

CONTACT INFORMATION

TWITTER: @MebFaber
EMAIL: Mebane@gmail.com
PHONE: 310-683-5500

BLOG: mebfaber.com
RESEARCH: theideafarm.com
COMPANY: cambriafunds.com

OTHER BOOKS BY MEB FABER

THE IVY PORTFOLIO
SHAREHOLDER YIELD
GLOBAL VALUE

{
However beautiful the strategy,
you should occasionally
look at the results.
}

WINSTON CHURCHILL

INTRODUCTION

To help put the reader in the right mindset for this book, let's run a little experiment. We want to make sure you're paying attention, so turn off the TV, close your email, and grab a cup of coffee.

Below is a test. It is simple, but requires your utmost concentration. Here is a video for you to watch. So click on this link and then come back to this book after watching—it's only about 20 seconds long so we'll wait.

Selective Attention Test Video[1]

Did you watch?

Okay, do you have your number? If you do your job correctly, you learn that the ball is passed 15 times. Did you get the number correct? Congratulations!

But, of course, that's not the whole story.

In this particular experiment, which many of you have probably seen already, while you were fastidiously counting basketball passes, what you might have missed was someone dressed in a gorilla costume walk into the frame, pound his chest, and walk

1   https://youtu.be/vJG698U2Mvo

off. Don't feel bad—most participants in the experiment don't notice the gorilla at all. While they kept their eye trained on what they assumed to be the most important task—the passing of the basketball—they simply failed to notice anything else.

Go back and watch again and be amazed that you would have missed this very obvious intruder. What the research actually finds is that when we narrow our focus to one specific task, we tend to overlook other, significant events.

What does this have to do with investing and this book? Conventional wisdom tells us that, as investors, we have to keep our eyes trained on our asset allocation. However, how much time do you spend thinking about the following questions:

"Is it the right time to be in stocks, or should I sell?"

"Should I add gold to my portfolio? If so, how much?"

"Aren't bonds in a bubble?"

"How much should I put in foreign stocks?"

"Are central banks manipulating the market?"

With all of our focus on assets—and how much and when to allocate them—are we missing the gorilla in the room?

Our book begins by reviewing the historical performance record of popular assets like stocks, bonds, and cash. We look at the impact inflation has on our money. We then start to examine how diversification through combining assets, in this case a simple stock and bond mix, works to mitigate the extreme drawdowns of risky asset classes.

But we go beyond a limited stock/bond portfolio to consider a more global allocation that also takes into account real assets. We track 13 assets and their returns since 1973, with particular attention to a number of well-known portfolios, like Ray Dalio's All Weather portfolio, the Endowment portfolio, Warren Buffett's suggestion, and others. And what we find is that, with a few notable exceptions, many of the allocations have similar exposures.

And yet, while we are all busy paying close attention to our portfolio's particular allocation of assets, the greatest impact on our portfolios may be something we fail to notice altogether. In this case, the so-called "gorilla" are the fees that we often fail to consider. In one shocking example, we find that the best performing strategy underperforms the worst strategy when we tack on advisory fees. Ultimately, smart investing requires that we not only monitor asset allocation, but of equal weight, we focus on the advisory fees associated with the investment strategy.

CHAPTER 1

A HISTORY OF STOCKS, BONDS, AND BILLS

Let's start with a history lesson. Many people begin investing their money without a true understanding of what has happened in the past, and often bias their expectations toward their own personal experiences. My mother always told me the way to invest was to buy some stocks and then just hold on to them. But her experience, living in the United States and investing particularly in the 1980s and 1990s, was very different from her parent's generation, which lived through the Great Depression. Both of these experiences would be vastly different from those of the average Japanese, German, or Russian investor.

So what is possible and reasonable to expect from history? We should begin with a discussion about the value of money.

A few years ago, my father and I were talking and he decided to demonstrate a real world example of inflation. A couple weeks later, I received a letter with a check inside written by my great grandfather in the 1910s for $0.50. He was a farmer who immigrated from Les Martigny-Baines, Voges France and ended up in

Nebraska. That $0.50 is equivalent to about $13 today and shows a very simple example of inflation. As a side note, look at that penmanship!

FIGURE 1   REAL WORLD INFLATION

Source: Faber

A more familiar example is the oft-used phrase, "I remember when a Coca-Cola cost ten cents." (Another fun example is "Superhero Inflation.")[1] Inflation is an emotional topic. It usually goes hand-in-hand with a discussion of The Federal Reserve, and there are not many topics that incite more vitriol in certain economic and political precincts than "The Fed" and the U.S. dollar.

One of the most famous charts in all of investing literature is the one below that illustrates the U.S. dollar's purchasing power since the creation of The Federal Reserve in 1913. The description usually goes along the lines of this ZeroHedge post:[2]

---

1   http://mebfaber.com/2013/07/29/superhero-inflation/
2   http://www.zerohedge.com/article/annihiliation-dollars-purchasing-power

*"This is the chart they don't want you to see: the purchasing power of the dollar over the past 76 years has **declined by 94%**. And based on current monetary and fiscal policy, we have at least another 94% to go. The only question is whether this will be achieved in 76 months this time."*

The above statement is factually true—$1.00 in 1913 is only worth about three cents in current dollars due to the effects of inflation (which have averaged about 3.2% a year). But that is all the chart tells you—the U.S. has had mild inflation this century (with fits of disinflation, deflation, and high inflation mixed in):

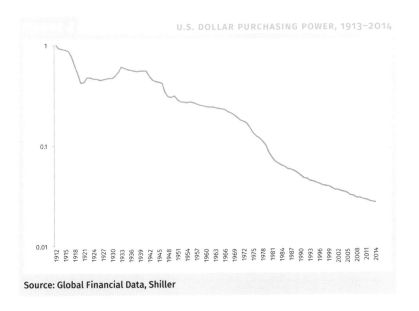

U.S. DOLLAR PURCHASING POWER, 1913–2014

Source: Global Financial Data, Shiller

The chart is then used to justify any number of arguments and conclusions, usually laden with exclamation points!!!, **bold text**, and CAPITALIZATIONS. Cries to end the Fed, buy gold, sell stocks, and build forts stocked with guns, food, and ammunition usually follow in a stream of rants and raves. These articles are written like this for a reason. They elicit an emotional response (who doesn't enjoy grumbling about the government?) and they certainly make for great headlines.

The problem that most miss is that investors have to do *something* with those dollars. Pretend you were an investor in 1913. You could choose to put your dollars under a mattress, in which case your purchasing power would decline as indicated in the chart above. You could also spend the money on consumption, such as vacations, entertainment, clothes, or food. Or you could invest in Treasury bills, in which case the dollar was a perfectly fine store of value, and your $1 would be worth $1.33 today (for a real return of about 0.26% per year).

So you didn't really make any money, but you were not losing any either.

Note that "real returns" refer to the returns an investor receives after inflation. If an investment returned 10% (what we call nominal returns) but there was inflation of 2% that year, the real return is only 8%. Real returns are a very important concept as they make comparisons across timeframes more relevant. A 10% return with 8% inflation (2% real) is very different than a 10% return with 2% inflation (8% real). It is helpful to think about real returns as "returns you can eat." That $1 Coke likely costs about the same as the $0.10 Coke, you are just paying with inflated dollars (and probably getting corn syrup instead of real sugar).

If you had decided to take on a little more risk, you could have invested in longer duration bonds, corporate bonds, gold, stocks, housing, or even wine and art—all of which would have been better stores of value than your mattress.

FIGURE 3 shows the real returns of stocks, bonds, and bills. While $1 would be worth only three cents had you put your hard-earned cash under the mattress, it would be worth $1.33 had you invested in T-bills, worth $5.68 in 10-Year Treasury bonds, and worth a whopping $492 in U.S. stocks.

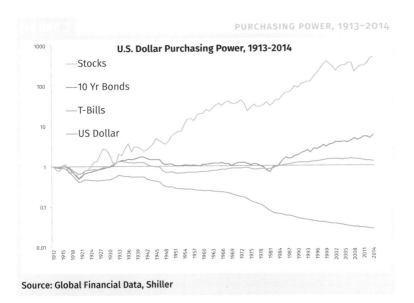

U.S. Dollar Purchasing Power, 1913-2014

— Stocks

— 10 Yr Bonds

— T-Bills

— US Dollar

Source: Global Financial Data, Shiller

For those looking for a beautiful coffee table book on the topic of historical market returns, check out my all-time favorite investing book, *Triumph of the Optimists: 101 Years of Global Investment Returns*.[1] (There are also free yearly updates of the book from Credit Suisse here.[2] All of the yearly updates are **highly** recommended.) This fantastic book illustrates that many global asset classes in the twentieth century produced nice gains in wealth for individuals who bought and held those assets for generation-long holding periods. It also shows how the assets went through regular and painful drawdowns like the Global Financial Crisis of 2008.

Unfortunately for investors, there are only two states for your portfolio—all-time highs and drawdowns. Drawdowns for those unfamiliar are simply the peak to trough loss you are experiencing in an investment. So if you bought an investment at 100 and

---

1   http://amzn.to/1zNnKZI
2   https://www.credit-suisse.com/us/en/news-and-expertise/research/
    credit-suisse-research-institute/publications.html

it declines to 75, you are in a 25% drawdown. If it then rises to 110, your drawdown is then 0 (all-time high).

For some long-term perspective, set forth below are some charts based on data from the book *Triumph of the Optimists* (available through Morningstar as the Dimson, Marsh, and Staunton module but requires a subscription). They represent the best-, middle-, and worst-case scenarios for the main asset classes of sixteen countries from 1900–2014. They have since updated their database to include 23 countries with results in the Credit Suisse reference link above. All return series are local real returns and displayed as a log graph (except the last one). U.S. dollar based returns are near identical.

First, here are the best-, middle-, and worst-cases for returns on your cash.

FIGURE 4 shows that leaving cash under your mattress is a slow bleed for a portfolio. Germany is excluded after the first series as it dominates the worst-case scenarios (in this case, hyperinflation). Inflation is a major drag on returns. When it gets out of control, it can completely wipe out your cash and bond savings. So you mattress stuffers—on average you would have lost about 4% a year by keeping your money at home.

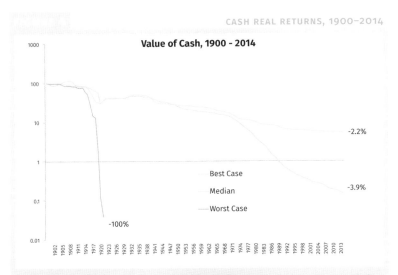

Value of Cash, 1900 - 2014

Best Case

Median

Worst Case

-2.2%

-3.9%

-100%

Source: Morningstar, Elroy Dimson, Paul Marsh, Mike Staunton, Triumph of the Optimists, Princeton University Press, 2002, Credit Suisse Global Investment Returns Sourcebook 2015

- Best-Case: -2.2% per year
- Middle: -3.9%
- Worst-Case: -100%

Next up are real returns for short-term government bills. These instruments do all they can just to keep up with inflation. You're not usually going to make any money, as FIGURE 5 shows, but at least they don't lose 4% a year like the mattress does. We also include the "World" which is the global market capitalization weighted portfolio which weights the portfolio based on size of each country's stock market.

FIGURE 5   SHORT-TERM GOVERNMENT BILLS REAL RETURNS 1900–2014

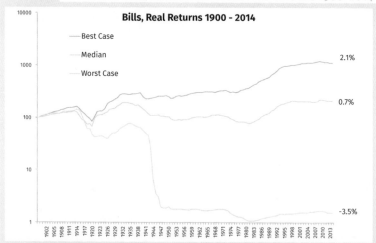

Bills, Real Returns 1900 - 2014

Source: Morningstar, Elroy Dimson, Paul Marsh, Mike Staunton, Triumph of the Optimists, Princeton University Press, 2002, Credit Suisse Global Investment Returns Sourcebook 2015

- Best-Case: 2.1% per year
- Middle: 0.7%
- Worst-Case: -3.5% (Real Worst-Case, Germany -100%)
- World: 0.9%

In FIGURE 6, adding a little duration risk doubles the historical returns of bills for our 10-year bonds, but that is still a pretty small return. You're not going to get rich with 1.7% real returns, and you still have to sit through a 50% drawdown, as we will show later.

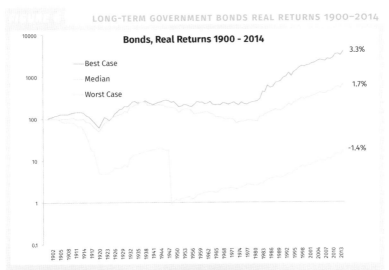

Bonds, Real Returns 1900 - 2014

Source: Morningstar, Elroy Dimson, Paul Marsh, Mike Staunton, Triumph of the Optimists, Princeton University Press, 2002, Credit Suisse Global Investment Returns Sourcebook 2015

- Best-Case: 3.3% per year
- Middle: 1.7%
- Worst-Case: -1.4% (Real Worst-Case, Germany -100%)
- World: 1.9%

And finally, we have the real returns for stocks. Much better! Over 4% real returns per year is far superior to returns of the bond market. While these are great returns, realize that it would still take over 15 years to double your money!

Source: Morningstar, Elroy Dimson, Paul Marsh, Mike Staunton, Triumph of the Optimists, Princeton University Press, 2002, Credit Suisse Global Investment Returns Sourcebook 2015

- Best-Case: 7.4% per year
- Middle: 4.8%
- Worst-Case: 1.9%
- (Real Worst-Case, China, Russia -100%)
- World: 5.2%

And in FIGURE 7A, the same chart is presented with a non-log y-axis. We do this to demonstrate to readers the importance of viewing charts that have percentage changes over long time frames with a log axis. Otherwise the chart is almost unreadable and definitely not useful. Perhaps importantly, you can now distinguish between unscrupulous money managers advertising their services with the below style of chart which can be misleading, as the gains look much more dramatic.

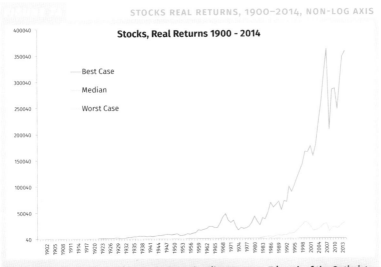

Source: Morningstar, Elroy Dimson, Paul Marsh, Mike Staunton, Triumph of the Optimists, Princeton University Press, 2002, Credit Suisse Global Investment Returns Sourcebook 2015

Let's look at the entire series across all countries to visualize some of the best and worst-case scenarios. It looks like a simple conservative rule of thumb may be to expect stocks to return around 4% to 5%, bonds 1% to 2%, and bills basically zero. Note that the United States had one of the best performing equity and bond markets for the 20th Century.

FIGURE 8 ASSET CLASS REAL RETURNS, 1900–2014

	INFLATION	BILLS	BONDS	EQUITY
Australia	3.8%	0.7%	1.7%	7.3%
Belgium	5.2%	-0.3%	0.4%	2.7%
Canada	3.0%	1.5%	2.2%	5.8%
Denmark	3.8%	2.1%	3.3%	5.3%
France	7.0%	-2.8%	0.2%	3.2%
Germany	*	-2.4%	-1.4%	3.2%
Ireland	4.2%	0.7%	1.6%	4.2%
Italy	8.2%	-3.5%	-1.2%	1.9%
Japan	6.8%	-1.9%	-0.9%	4.1%
Netherlands	2.9%	0.6%	1.7%	5.0%
South Africa	4.9%	1.0%	1.9%	7.4%
Spain	5.7%	0.3%	1.8%	3.7%
Sweden	3.5%	1.9%	2.8%	5.8%
Switzerland	2.2%	0.8%	2.3%	4.5%
UK	3.9%	0.9%	1.6%	5.3%
US	2.9%	0.9%	2.0%	6.5%
Max	8.2%	2.1%	3.3%	7.4%
Median	3.9%	0.7%	1.7%	4.8%
Average	4.5%	0.0%	1.3%	4.7%
Min	2.2%	-3.5%	-1.4%	1.9%

Source: Morningstar, Elroy Dimson, Paul Marsh, Mike Staunton, Triumph of the Optimists, Princeton University Press, 2002, Credit Suisse Global Investment Returns Sourcebook 2015

One would think that the math above would make the decision easy—just put all your money in stocks! While stocks outperformed the returns of bonds and bills, stocks are not without their own risks. At least two countries had their equity markets wiped out when the government shut down the capital markets. No wonder people are so wary of investing in Russia and China even today.

Another risk is that stocks can go for a really long time

underperforming other asset classes, such as bonds. It is easy to look at the data and assume you can wait out any stock market underperformance—at least until it happens to you.

In his 2011 "The Biggest Urban Legend in Finance," [1] Rob Arnott discusses a 30-year underperformance of stocks vs. bonds:

"A 30-year stock market excess return of approximately zero is a huge disappointment to the legions of "stocks at any price" long-term investors. But it's not the first extended drought. From 1803 to 1857, U.S. equities struggled; the stock investor would have received a third of the ending wealth of the bond investor. Stocks managed to break even only in 1871. Most observers would be shocked to learn there was ever a 68-year stretch of stock market underperformance. After a 72-year bull market from 1857 through 1929, another dry spell ensued. From 1929 through 1949, stocks failed to match bonds, the only long-term shortfall in the Ibbotson time sample. Perhaps it was the extraordinary period of history—The Great Depression and World War II—and the spectacular aftermath from 1950– 1999, that lulled recent investors into a false sense of security regarding long-term equity performance."

A 68-year long stock underperformance is almost the same as a human's current expected lifespan in the U.S. Bonds outperformed stocks over an entire lifetime (really, more than a lifetime, since life expectancy in the 1800s was around 40 years in the U.S.). When talking about stocks for the long run, then, it must mean something other than a human lifetime. For a tortoise, deep sea tubeworm, or sequoia tree perhaps? To be fair, the longer you go back in history the more suspect the data is, so we confine our analysis below to the post 1900 period.

Other countries experienced large drawdowns, and even in

---

1   https://www.researchaffiliates.com/Our Ideas/Insights/Fundamentals/
    Pages/F_2011_March_The_Biggest_Urban_Legend.aspx

the United States, an investor lost about 80% from the peak in the 1929–1930s stock bear market. The unfortunate mathematics of a 75% decline requires an investor to realize a 300% gain just to get back to even—the equivalent of compounding at 4.8% for 30 years! Even a smaller 50% drawdown would require 15 years at that rate of return to get back to even.

Large drawdowns are why many people choose to invest in bonds, but bonds are risky too. While stocks typically suffer from sharper price declines, bonds often have their value eroded by inflation. The U.S. and the U.K. have both seen real bond drawdowns of over 60%. While that sounds painful, in many other countries (Japan, Germany, Italy, and France), it was worse than 80%. Some countries that faced hyperinflation resulted in a total loss, and Business Insider has a slideshow[1] that examines a few of the worst examples in the past 100 years.

FIGURE 9 shows that both stocks and bonds have had multiple large drawdowns over the years. The first chart uses monthly data (we don't have monthly for the U.K.), and monthly data only increases the drawdown figure.

The same principle occurs in the U.K., but bond investors had to wait even longer to get back to even—almost 50 years! Below is FIGURE 10 looking at yearly real returns and drawdowns.

1   www.businessinsider.com/worst-hyperinflation-episodes-in-history-2013-9

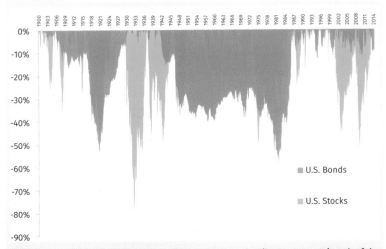

Source: Morningstar, Bloomberg, Elroy Dimson, Paul Marsh, Mike Staunton, Triumph of the Optimists, Princeton University Press 2002

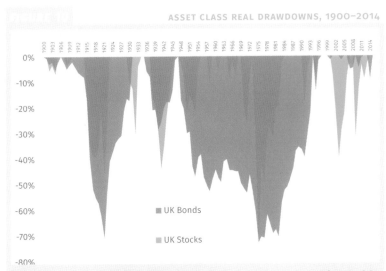

Source: Morningstar, Bloomberg, Elroy Dimson, Paul Marsh, Mike Staunton, Triumph of the Optimists, Princeton University Press 2002

This is one of the problems with investing in just one security, country, or asset class. Normal market returns are extreme. Individuals invested in various assets at specific periods—U.S. stocks in the late 1920s and early 1930s, German asset classes in the 1910s and 1940s, Russian stocks in 1917, Chinese stocks in 1949, U.S. real estate in the mid-1950s, Japanese stocks in the 1990s, emerging markets and commodities in the late 1990s, and nearly everything in 2008—would reason that holding these assets was a decidedly unwise course of action. Most individuals do not have a sufficiently long time to recover from large drawdowns from any one risky asset class.

So what is an investor to do? The next step lies in what is called the only free lunch in investing—diversification.

CHAPTER 2

THE BENCHMARK PORTFOLIO: 60/40

"No strategy is so good that it can't have a bad year or more. You've got to guess at worst cases: No model will tell you that. My rule of thumb is double the worst that you have ever seen."

— CLIFF ASNESS, CO-FOUNDER AQR
CAPITAL MANAGEMENT

The most venerable asset allocation model is the traditional 60/40 portfolio. The portfolio simply invests 60% in stocks (S&P 500) and 40% in 10-year U.S. government bonds. We will use this portfolio as the benchmark to compare all of the following portfolios in this book.

The reason many people will invest in both stocks and bonds is that they are often non-correlated, meaning, stocks often zig while bonds zag. While the relationship isn't constant, combining two or more non-correlated assets into a portfolio results in a better portfolio than just either alone.

How has this portfolio performed? Let's look at the U.S. 60/40 portfolio back to 1913, rebalanced monthly. We consider volatility to be measured by the standard deviation of monthly returns. The Sharpe ratio is a measure of risk adjusted returns, and is calculated as: (returns−risk free rate)/volatility. The risk-free rate is simply the return of Treasury bills. A higher Sharpe ratio is better, and a good rule of thumb is that risky asset classes have Sharpe ratios that cluster around the 0.20 to 0.30 range.

FIGURE 11	ASSET CLASS REAL RETURNS, 1913–2013		
	BONDS	STOCKS	60/40
Returns	1.82%	6.59%	5.11%
Volatility	6.68%	18.61%	11.79%
Sharpe	0.22	0.33	0.40
Max Drawdown	-59.06%	-78.94%	-52.38%

Source: Global Financial Data

FIGURE 12 — ASSET CLASS REAL RETURNS, 1913–2013

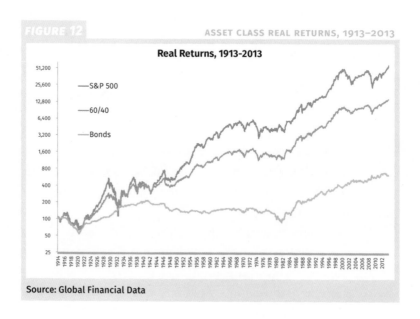

Source: Global Financial Data

So it looks like you get a nice diversification benefit of investing your portfolio in both assets. While 60/40 doesn't quite achieve the returns of stocks, you reduce your drawdown a bit due to the assets not being perfectly correlated. FIGURE 12 shows the equity curve of the strategy.

One challenge for investors is how much time they spend in drawdowns. It is emotionally challenging, largely, since we anchor to the highest value a portfolio has attained. For example, if your account hit $100,000 last month up from $20,000 twenty years ago, you likely think of your wealth in terms of the recent value and not the original $20,000. If it then declines to $80,000, most will think in terms of losing $20,000 rather than the long-term gain of $60,000. The 60/40 allocation only spends about 22% of the time at new highs, and the other 78% in some degree of drawdown. Drawdowns are physically painful, and the behavioral research demonstrates that people hate losing money much more than the joy of similar gains. To be a good (read: patient) investor you need to be able to sit through the dry spells.

So why not just allocate to the 60/40 portfolio and avoid reading the rest of this book?

While 60/40 is a solid first step, we posit that focusing solely on U.S. stocks and bonds is a mistake. In fact, this 60/40 approach presents a particularly difficult challenge to investors at the end of 2014, as we detail below.

U.S. stocks have returned a meager 4.9% per year from 2000–2014 and, factoring in inflation, have returned 1.90% per year, provided investors had the ability to sit through two gut-wrenching bear markets with declines of over 45%. According to recent DALBAR studies,[1] many have not. 1.9% per year is a far cry from the historical 6.47% that U.S. stocks have returned over the full period from 1900–2014.

1   http://www.qaib.com/public/default.aspx

One of the reasons for the subpar returns is simple—valuations matter. The price you pay influences your rate of return. Pay a below average price and you can reasonably expect an above average return, and vice versa. Valuations started the 2000s at extreme levels. The ten-year cyclically adjusted price-to-earnings (CAPE) ratio for U.S. stocks reached a level of 45 in December 1999, the highest level ever recorded in the U.S., as FIGURE 13 shows. (For those unfamiliar with valuation methods for stocks, we examine over 40 global stock markets and how to use global valuation metrics in our book *Global Value*.) This high starting valuation set the stage for very poor returns going forward for investors buying stocks in the late 1990s.

As you can see in the FIGURE 14, future returns are highly dependent on those starting valuations. The current reading as of December 2014 is 27, which is about 60% above the long-term average of around 16.5. At the current levels over 25, future median ten-year returns have been an uninspiring 3.5% nominal and 1.00% real since 1900. Not horrific and not quite yet in a bubble—but not that exciting either. Once CAPE ratios rise above 30, forecasted future median real returns are negative for the following ten years—it doesn't make sense to overpay for stocks!

U.S. 10-year government bonds, on the other hand, have proven to be a wonderful place to invest during the past 15 years. The compound return was 6.24% and a nice 3.82% after inflation. The problem here, however, is that these wonderful recent returns come at the expense of future returns as yields have declined from around 6% in 2000 to near all-time low levels in the U.S., currently around 2%.

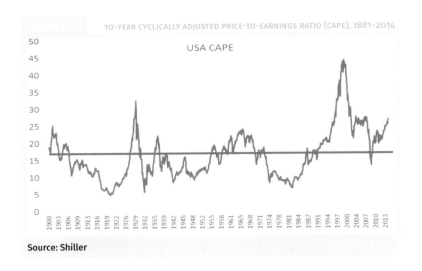

USA CAPE

Source: Shiller

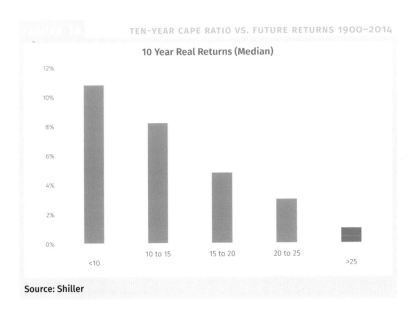

10 Year Real Returns (Median)

Source: Shiller

Future bond returns are fairly easy to forecast—each future bond return is simply the starting yield. Currently, your ten-year nominal return for buying U.S. government bonds will be around 2.25% if held to maturity.

So investors are presented with the following opportunity set of annual returns for the next ten years (assuming 2.25% inflation going forward, rounding to make it simple):

- U.S. Stocks: 3.50% nominal, ~1% real
- U.S. Bonds: 2.25% nominal, ~0% real
- Cash/T-bills: 0.00% nominal, -2% real

That leaves a 60/40 investor with a 2–3% nominal return no matter which way you slice it, or about a 0–1% real return. Not exactly breathtaking! Many investors expect 8% (or even 10% returns) per year when, in reality, expectations should be ratcheted down to more reasonable levels.

Other highly respected research shops forecast similar bleak returns for U.S. stocks and bonds. You can find more info at AQR,[1] Bridgewater,[2] Research Affiliates,[3] and GMO.[4]

So where should investors look for returns while minimizing their risk of overpaying? In the coming pages, we examine the benefits of expanding a traditional 60/40 allocation into a more global allocation with an additional focus on real assets as well.

1   https://www.aqr.com/library
2   http://www.bwater.com/
3   http://www.researchaffiliates.com/AssetAllocation/Pages/Core-Overview.aspx
4   http://www.gmo.com/

CHAPTER 3

ASSET CLASS BUILDING BLOCKS

"I think the single most important thing that you can do is diversify your portfolio."

— PAUL TUDOR JONES, FOUNDER TUDOR
INVESTMENT CORPORATION

The next two questions and answers will likely surprise you.

Question 1—Quick, what is the world's largest financial asset class? Don't know?

Answer: Foreign ex-U.S. bonds! This is usually surprising to most investors who assume the answer is U.S. stocks or bonds.

Question 2: How much of your global stock allocation should be in the United States?

Answer: About half!

U.S. investors usually put around 70% of their stock allocation at home here in the U.S. This is called the "home country bias", and it occurs everywhere. Most investors around the world invest most of their assets in their own markets.

Non–U.S. bonds are the world's largest asset class

Global investable market components, 1995 – March 2013

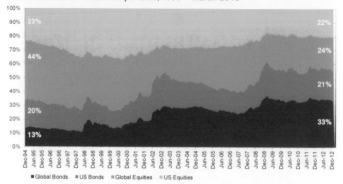

Notes: Global bonds are represented by the Barclays Capital Global Aggregate ex-USD Bond Index through July 2001 and by that index plus the Barclays Capital Global Emerging Markets Index thereafter. U.S. bonds are represented by the Barclays Capital U.S. Aggregate Bond Index. U.S. stocks are represented by the MSCI USA Investable Market Index. Global equities are represented by the MSCI All-Country World Investable Market Index ex USA.
Sources: Thomson Reuters Datastream, Barclays Capital, MSCI and Vanguard. Data through March 31, 2013.
FOR FINANCIAL ADVISORS AND INSTITUTIONS ONLY. NOT FOR PUBLIC DISTRIBUTION.   11

Source: Vanguard

Source: Vanguard

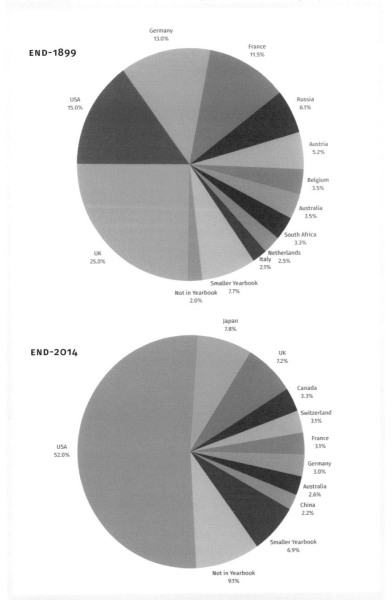

END-1899

Germany 13.0%
France 11.5%
USA 15.0%
Russia 6.1%
Austria 5.2%
Belgium 3.5%
Australia 3.5%
South Africa 3.3%
UK 25.0%
Netherlands 2.5%
Italy 2.1%
Smaller Yearbook 7.7%
Not in Yearbook 2.0%

END-2014

Japan 7.8%
UK 7.2%
Canada 3.3%
Switzerland 3.1%
France 3.1%
Germany 3.0%
Australia 2.6%
China 2.2%
USA 52.0%
Smaller Yearbook 6.9%
Not in Yearbook 9.1%

Source: Elroy Dimson, Paul Marsh, Mike Staunton, Triumph of the Optimists, Princeton University Press 2002, Credit Suisse Global Investment Returns Sourcebook 2015

FIGURE 16 is a chart from Vanguard that details the "home country bias" effect in the U.S., the U.K., Australia, and Canada. The blue bars are how much investors should own of each country according to global weightings, and the red bars are how much they actually own of their own country—way too much!

FIGURE 17 is a chart from the Credit Suisse GIRY update we mentioned earlier. It details the U.S. as a percentage of world market capitalization (52%) in 2014. Given this, while most of us here in the United States invest 70% of our stock allocation in U.S. stocks, in order to be truly representative of the global marketplace it really should only be about half. Note that the U.S. was only 15% of world market cap back in 1899. As a share of global GDP, the U.S. is only 20% (emerging markets are 50% of global GDP, but only 13% of market capitalization).

The point of the two questions at the beginning of the chapter is that we live in a global world. There is no need to build an investment portfolio with just exposure to U.S. stocks and bonds. FIGURE 18 is another chart of how market cap weightings have changed over time. Notice the large Japanese bubble expansion in the 1980s and the rapid contraction afterward.

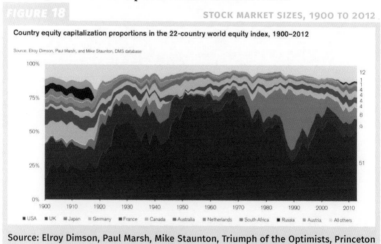

FIGURE 18   STOCK MARKET SIZES, 1900 TO 2012

Country equity capitalization proportions in the 22-country world equity index, 1900–2012

Source: Elroy Dimson, Paul Marsh, and Mike Staunton, DMS database

Source: Elroy Dimson, Paul Marsh, Mike Staunton, Triumph of the Optimists, Princeton University Press 2002, Credit Suisse Global Investment Returns Sourcebook

The key question for investors to ask, then, is, "What would our allocation look like if we expanded the 60/40 portfolio to include foreign stocks and bonds? Would that help improve our returns or reduce our risk?"

THE GLOBAL 60-40 PORTFOLIO

The next portfolio we will examine is the 60/40 portfolio, only now we are using global indices rather than just U.S. ones. We split the stock allocation into half domestic and half foreign developed stocks (MSCI EAFE), and split the bond allocation into half domestic and half foreign 10-year government bonds.

Going global in this illustration doesn't change the end result too much, though it does increase returns, reduce volatility, and improve the Sharpe ratio (all good things). The global portfolio also did better during the inflationary 1973–1981 period, as FIGURE 19 shows.

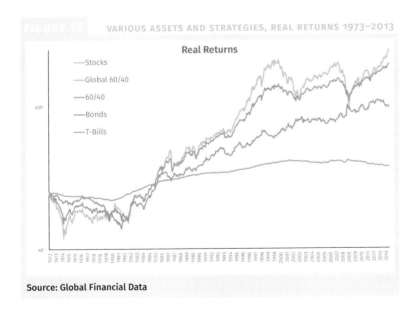

VARIOUS ASSETS AND STRATEGIES, REAL RETURNS 1973–2013

Source: Global Financial Data

NOMINAL RETURNS 1973-2013

	T-BILLS	BONDS	STOCKS	60/40	GLOBAL 60/40
Returns	5.27%	7.74%	10.21%	9.60%	10.02%
Volatility	0.97%	8.43%	15.57%	10.20%	9.90%
Sharpe	0.00	0.29	0.32	0.42	0.48
Max Drawdown	0.00%	-15.79%	-50.95%	-29.28%	-35.20%

REAL RETURNS 1973-2013

	T-BILLS	BONDS	STOCKS	60/40	GLOBAL 60/40
Returns	0.99%	3.34%	5.71%	5.13%	5.54%
Volatility	1.24%	8.73%	15.74%	10.46%	10.14%
Sharpe	0.00	0.27	0.30	0.39	0.45
Max Drawdown	0.00%	-44.75%	-54.12%	-39.35%	-36.74%

REAL RETURNS 1973-1981

	T-BILLS	BONDS	STOCKS	60/40	GLOBAL 60/40
Returns	-0.71%	-5.08%	-3.92%	-4.05%	-2.09%

REAL RETURNS 1982-2013

	T-BILLS	BONDS	STOCKS	60/40	GLOBAL 60/40
Returns	1.48%	5.85%	8.61%	7.88%	7.80%

REAL RETURNS 1973-2013

	T-BILLS	BONDS	STOCKS	60/40	GLOBAL 60/40
1970s	-1.55%	-4.23%	-5.26%	-4.56%	-1.98%
1980s	3.81%	7.22%	11.67%	10.28%	11.37%
1990s	1.95%	4.87%	14.71%	10.89%	8.88%
2000s	0.19%	3.92%	-3.38%	-0.04%	1.67%
2010s	-1.82%	2.17%	13.73%	9.44%	6.36%
Volatility	2.38%	4.33%	9.78%	7.05%	5.41%

Source: Global Financial Data

There is no reason, however for investors to focus exclusively on stocks and bonds. Would increasing amounts of granularity with additional asset classes help when looking at building a diversified portfolio? In this book, we are going to examine 13 assets and their returns since 1973. They are found in FIGURE 20 below with a column denoting what broad category of assets they fall under.

		ASSET CLASSES
US Large Cap	Stocks	S&P 500
US Small Cap	Stocks	French Fama Small Cap
Foreign Developed	Stocks	MSCI EAFE
Foreign Emerging	Stocks	MSCI EEM
Corporate Bonds	Stocks/Bonds	Dow Jones Corporate
T-Bills	Bonds	U.S. bills
10 Year Bonds	Bonds	U.S. 10-year bonds
30 Year Bonds	Bonds	U.S. 30-year bonds
10 Year Foreign Bonds	Bonds	Foreign 10-year bonds
TIPS	Real Assets	Barclays
Commodities	Real Assets	GSCI
Gold	Real Assets	GFD
REITs	Real Assets	NAREIT

Are there other asset classes? Of course. However, many asset classes (or sub-asset classes) do not have sufficient histories to analyze, such as emerging market bonds. For those unfamiliar, REITS are publicly traded real estate investment trusts, and TIPS are U.S. Treasury inflation protected bonds.[1]

We also exclude active approaches to investing even though we discuss some of these "tilts" in other white papers and books like *Shareholder Yield*. So while an active strategy like managed

---

1   https://www.treasurydirect.gov/indiv/products/prod_tips_glance.htm

futures is one of my favorite investment strategies, we don't include it in the building blocks section. (I like to call trendfollowing my "desert island" strategy if I had to pick one method to manage money for the rest of my life. While not the topic of this book, we have written a great deal about trend strategies on the blog as well as in the white paper "A Quantitative Approach to Tactical Asset Allocation.")[1]

FIGURE 21 presents a chart of the asset classes we examine in the following chapters.

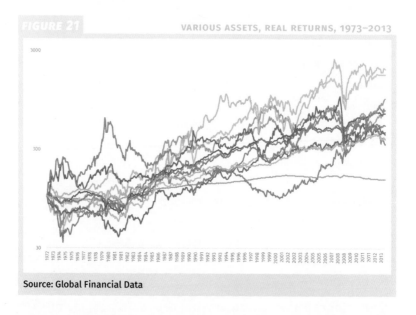

FIGURE 21   VARIOUS ASSETS, REAL RETURNS, 1973–2013

Source: Global Financial Data

We didn't label the asset classes in the chart on purpose simply to demonstrate that while the indexes traveled different routes from start to finish, all of the asset classes finished with positive real returns over the time period. The fact that bonds were even close in absolute performance to the other equity-like asset classes reflects the greater than thirty-year bull market that took yields

1   http://papers.ssrn.com/sol3/papers.cfm?abstract_id=962461

from double-digit levels to near 2% today. The charts on the next page demonstrate the returns and risk characteristics of the various asset classes.

While these are some pretty nice returns for these asset classes historically, they suffered through some large drawdowns.

Like we discussed before, nominal returns are illusory. You can't spend or eat nominal returns. In FIGURE 23 are the same building blocks but with real returns. Stocks were in the ballpark of 5–7%, bonds 0–5%, and real assets 3–5%. (Corporate bonds share equity-like characteristics, so we characterize them as 50% stocks and 50% bonds for purposes later in the paper.)

If an investor were to take the data back further, or use daily data observations, those drawdowns only get bigger. It is a sad fact that as an investor, you are either at an all-time high with your portfolio or in a drawdown—there is no middle ground—and the largest absolute drawdown will always be in your future as the number can only grow larger. (Unless you went bankrupt of course as then the amount is a total loss. Sadly, Brazil's richest man experienced this event when he lost over $30 billion—here is a good article on the topic[2] with lots of lessons for individuals as well.)

One of the biggest challenges of investing is that any asset can have a long period of underperformance relative to other assets—or even outright negative returns and losses. Cliff Asness, co-founder of AQR Capital Management, has a fun piece out on his blog titled "Efficient Frontier 'Theory' for the Long Run,"[3] where he talks about five-year periods in stocks, bonds, and commodities and basically how anything can happen over short periods of time. (Although for many investors, five years can feel like a lifetime.)

2 http://mebfaber.com/2013/10/05/the-big-mistake/
3 https://www.aqr.com/cliffs-perspective/efficient-frontier-theory-for-the-long-run

FIGURE 22

	US LARGE	US SMALL	FOREIGN EAFE	FOREIGN EEM	CORP. BONDS	T-BILLS
Returns	10.21%	11.71%	9.49%	12.05%	9.29%	5.27%
Volatility	15.57%	18.90%	17.49%	22.05%	6.62%	0.97%
Sharpe	0.32	0.34	0.24	0.31	0.61	0.00
Max Drawdown	-50.95%	-51.93%	-56.40%	-61.44%	-20.08%	0.00%

FIGURE 23

	US LARGE	US SMALL	FOREIGN EAFE	FOREIGN EEM	CORP. BONDS	T-BILLS
Returns	5.71%	7.16%	5.03%	7.50%	4.84%	0.99%
Volatility	15.74%	19.04%	17.65%	22.11%	6.97%	1.24%
Sharpe	0.30	0.32	0.23	0.29	0.55	-0.00
Max Drawdown	-54.12%	-60.01%	-57.07%	-61.98%	-39.17%	-12.54%

FIGURE 24

	US LARGE	US SMALL	FOREIGN EAFE	FOREIGN EEM	CORP. BONDS	T-BILLS
1973-1981	-3.92%	1.43%	-1.22%	4.29%	-3.79%	-0.71%
1982-2013	8.61%	8.85%	6.87%	8.45%	7.41%	1.48%
1970s	-5.26%	-0.05%	-1.59%	5.05%	-2.05%	-1.55%
1980s	11.67%	11.72%	16.65%	11.58%	9.20%	3.81%
1990s	14.71%	12.27%	4.22%	7.82%	5.50%	1.95%
2000s	-3.38%	2.49%	-0.92%	7.33%	4.93%	0.19%
2010s	13.73%	8.11%	6.49%	1.16%	4.47%	-1.82%
Volatility	9.78%	5.51%	7.37%	3.83%	4.07%	2.38%

Source: Global Financial Data

US 10 YEAR	US 30 YEAR	FOREIGN 10YR	TIPS	GSCI	REITS	GOLD
7.74%	8.03%	8.54%	7.66%	8.08%	9.49%	7.36%
8.43%	12.84%	7.52%	6.32%	20.37%	18.05%	20.88%
0.29	0.21	0.43	0.38	0.14	0.23	0.10
-15.79%	-25.84%	-15.21%	-11.89%	-67.65%	-67.88%	-64.97%

ASSET CLASS REAL RETURNS, 1973-2013

US 10 YEAR	US 30 YEAR	FOREIGN 10YR	TIPS	GSCI	REITS	GOLD
3.34%	3.60%	4.12%	3.29%	3.73%	5.03%	3.01%
8.73%	13.21%	7.76%	6.40%	20.19%	18.18%	20.77%
0.27	0.20	0.40	0.36	0.14	0.22	0.10
-44.75%	-61.18%	-32.68%	-22.33%	-66.40%	-69.26%	-84.59%

ASSET CLASS RETURNS, 1973-2013

US 10 YEAR	US 30 YEAR	FOREIGN 10YR	TIPS	GSCI	REITS	GOLD
-5.08%	-8.65%	-2.66%	0.49%	3.27%	-2.28%	13.02%
5.85%	7.34%	6.13%	4.10%	3.87%	7.19%	0.37%
-4.23%	-7.64%	-0.84%	0.83%	9.66%	-4.58%	25.45%
7.22%	7.89%	6.48%	4.49%	5.23%	6.98%	-7.57%
4.87%	5.98%	6.95%	2.38%	0.95%	4.97%	-6.71%
3.92%	5.11%	4.09%	5.03%	2.58%	7.45%	11.40%
2.17%	4.13%	0.13%	2.40%	-0.33%	12.00%	0.49%
4.33%	6.16%	3.58%	1.72%	3.96%	6.12%	13.91%

Using the data in FIGURE 24, we examine returns during two periods, inflationary 1973–1981 and falling inflation/disinflation 1982–2013. We also look at asset returns by decade. The final line in the table is the volatility of *decade* returns. While there are only five observations its helps to demonstrate the decade level consistency.

What can we learn from these tables? All of our assets had positive real returns, which is what you want from investing in any asset.

Real returns were much harder to come by in the inflationary 1970s. Eight out of 13 asset classes had negative real returns in the 1970s. Gold, commodities, and emerging market stocks had the best performance. Everything was up big in the 1982–2013 timeframe, but gold and cash lagged the most as the transition from high interest rates and inflation led to growth, lower inflation, and lower still interest rates. The only asset classes that had positive performance in every decade were emerging markets and TIPS, although the TIPS category is not a completely fair comparison since they were only introduced in 1997 and therefore this is a synthetic series that investors could not have allocated to at the time.

While there are certainly hundreds of different portfolios one can construct from our 13 assets, we are going to focus on just a handful of allocations below. (More "lazy portfolio" ideas here.)[1] These allocations have been proposed by some of the most famous money managers in the world, collectively managing hundreds of billions of dollars. We included a few other portfolios worthy of mention in the Appendix, but excluded them from the body of the text to keep things simple. Otherwise this book could have easily been 300 pages and the goal is not to put you to sleep but rather let you finish in one sitting and get on with your life.

The flow of the chapters will range from the portfolios that allocate the most to bonds to the ones that allocate the least.

Let's get started!

1   http://www.bogleheads.org/wiki/Lazy_portfolios

CHAPTER 4

THE RISK PARITY AND ALL SEASONS PORTFOLIOS

"I know that there are good and bad environments for all asset classes. And I know that in one's lifetime, there will be a ruinous environment for one of those asset classes. That's been true throughout history."

— RAY DALIO, FOUNDER BRIDGEWATER ASSOCIATES

"Today we can structure a portfolio that will do well in 2022, even though we can't possibly know what the world will look like in 2022."

— BOB PRINCE, CO-CIO BRIDGEWATER ASSOCIATES

Risk parity is a term that focuses on building a portfolio based on allocating weights based on "risk" rather than dollar weights in the portfolio. While the general theory of risk parity isn't something particularly new, the term was only coined within the past decade and became in vogue in the past few years. Risk is defined in different ways but volatility is a simple example. As an illustration, the 60/40 stocks and bonds portfolio doesn't have 60% of total overall risk weighted to stocks, rather, more like 90% since stock volatility dominates the portfolio's overall total volatility.

Risk parity has its roots in the modern portfolio theory of Harry Markowitz. While introduced in the 1950s, it eventually earned him a Nobel Prize. The basic theory suggested the concept of an efficient frontier—the allocation that offers the highest return for any given level of risk, and vice versa. When combined with the work of Tobin, Treynor, Sharpe, and others the theory demonstrates that a portfolio could be leveraged or deleveraged to target desired risk and return parameters. Many commodity trading advisors (CTAs) have also been using risk- or volatility-level position-sizing methods since at least the 1980s.

Ray Dalio's Bridgewater, one of the largest hedge funds in the world based on assets under management, was likely the first to launch a true risk parity portfolio in 1996 called All Weather. Many firms have since launched risk parity products. While the underlying construction methods are different, the broad theory is generally the same.

We are not going to focus too much on risk parity since Bridgewater and others have published extensively on the topic, and you will find several links at the end of this chapter. Three primer papers to read are "The All Weather Story," "The Biggest Mistake in Investing," and "Engineering Targeted Returns and Risks"— all of which can be found on the Bridgewater[1] website.

Bridgewater describes the theory in their white paper "The All Weather Story":

"All Weather grew out of Bridgewater's effort to make sense of the world, to hold the portfolio today that will do reasonably well 20 years from now even if no one can predict what form of growth and inflation will prevail.

---

1   http://www.bwater.com/

When investing over the long run, all you can have confidence in is that (1) holding assets should provide a return above cash, and (2) asset volatility will be largely driven by how economic conditions unfold relative to current expectations (as well as how these expectations change). That's it. Anything else (asset class returns, correlations, or even precise volatilities) is an attempt to predict the future. In essence, All Weather can be sketched out on a napkin. It is as simple as holding four different portfolios each with the same risk, each of which does well in a particular environment: when (1) inflation rises, (2) inflation falls, (3) growth rises, and (4) growth falls relative to expectations."

In another piece, "Engineering Targeted Returns and Risks", Dalio refers to the simple building blocks he calls market betas (such as U.S. stocks or bonds):

"Betas are limited in number (that is, not many viable asset classes exist), they are typically relatively correlated with each other, and their excess returns are relatively low compared to their excess risks, with Sharpe ratios typically ranging from 0.2 to 0.3. However, betas are reliable—we can expect they will outperform cash over long time horizons."

Investors need not view any single asset class in its prepackaged form, meaning, leveraging any single asset class, like bonds, can result in higher returns along with volatility similar to stocks. Many asset classes come with embedded leverage already, and adjusting to a risk level by leveraging or deleveraging assets is neither good nor evil—it just is. (A simple example is that many companies carry debt, so one could view stocks as leveraged already.) More from "The All Weather Story":

"Low-risk/low-return assets can be converted into high-risk/high-return assets. Translation: when viewed in terms of return per unit of risk, all assets are more or less the same. Investing in bonds, when risk-adjusted to *stock-like risk, didn't require an investor to sacrifice return in the service of diversification. This made sense. Investors should basically be compensated in proportion to the risk they take on: the more risk, the higher the reward."*

Combining assets with similar volatility into a portfolio results in a total allocation with more in low-volatility assets (like bonds) and less to high-volatility assets (like stocks).

Many other firms now offer risk parity strategies, and you can track a risk parity index[1] from Salient Partners. There are a handful of risk parity mutual funds from firms such as AQR, Putnam, and Invesco, although most are very expensive. A risk parity ETF was filed by Global X but never launched. The theory is well accepted and adopted by a large cadre of the investment community, but the key question is—"has this strategy simply ridden the wave of a secular trend downward in interest rates?" Only time will tell.

Below we examine two variations of risk parity. The first is a risk parity portfolio we proposed back in 2012 while giving a speech in New York City that reflects a broad risk parity style of investing (FIGURE 25).

Why try to divine the actual risk parity allocation when we can just go straight to the source and let Mr. Dalio construct it for us? The second allocation is the "All Seasons" portfolio Dalio himself suggested in the recent Tony Robbins book *Master the Money Game*[2] (FIGURE 26).

So how did these two portfolios perform? Almost identically, which isn't surprising due to the similar nature of the allocation.

1   http://www.salientindices.com/
2   http://amzn.to/1CK9gNO

US Large Cap	Stocks	8%
US Small Cap	Stocks	
Foreign Developed	Stocks	8%
Foreign Emerging	Stocks	
Corporate Bonds	Stocks/Bonds	35%
T-Bills	Bonds	
10 Year Bonds	Bonds	35%
30 Year Bonds	Bonds	
10 Year Foreign Bonds	Bonds	
TIPS	Real Assets	
Commodities	Real Assets	5%
Gold	Real Assets	5%
REITs	Real Assets	5%

Source: Faber PPT, 2012

US Large Cap	Stocks	18%
US Small Cap	Stocks	3%
Foreign Developed	Stocks	6%
Foreign Emerging	Stocks	3%
Corporate Bonds	Stocks/Bonds	
T-Bills	Bonds	
10 Year Bonds	Bonds	15%
30 Year Bonds	Bonds	40%
10 Year Foreign Bonds	Bonds	
TIPS	Real Assets	
Commodities	Real Assets	8%
Gold	Real Assets	8%
REITs	Real Assets	

Source: Master the Money Game, 2014

FIGURE 27

Source: Global Financial Data

In general, the theory behind risk parity makes a lot of sense with one caveat—the biggest challenge to a risk parity portfolio *now* is that we are potentially near the end of a 30-year bull market in bonds. The returns of the actual All Weather fund are better than the allocations above since Bridgewater uses leverage (which is essentially borrowing money to invest more thus magnifying both gains and losses). You can find a blog post comparing the returns of All Weather to a leveraged Global Asset Allocation portfolio in my article "Cloning the Largest Hedge Fund in the World."[1]

---

1   http://mebfaber.com/2014/12/31/
    cloning-the-largest-hedge-fund-in-the-world-bridgewaters-all-weather/

	T-BILLS	BONDS	STOCKS	ALL SEASONS	RISK PARITY
Returns	5.27%	7.74%	10.21%	9.50%	9.21%
Volatility	0.97%	8.43%	15.57%	8.24%	6.48%
Sharpe	0.00	0.29	0.32	0.51	0.61
Max Drawdown	0.00%	-15.79%	-50.95%	-14.59%	-14.41%

REAL RETURNS 1973-2013

	T-BILLS	BONDS	STOCKS	ALL SEASONS	RISK PARITY
Returns	0.99%	3.34%	5.71%	5.04%	4.76%
Volatility	1.24%	8.73%	15.74%	8.56%	6.78%
Sharpe	0.00	0.27	0.30	0.47	0.56
Max Drawdown	0.00%	-44.75%	-54.12%	-28.77%	-24.77%

REAL RETURNS 1973-1981

	T-BILLS	BONDS	STOCKS	ALL SEASONS	RISK PARITY
Returns	-0.71%	-5.08%	-3.92%	-2.83%	-2.20%

REAL RETURNS 1982-2013

	T-BILLS	BONDS	STOCKS	ALL SEASONS	RISK PARITY
Returns	1.48%	5.85%	8.61%	7.38%	6.82%

REAL RETURNS 1973-2013

	T-BILLS	BONDS	STOCKS	ALL SEASONS	RISK PARITY
1970s	-1.55%	-4.23%	-5.26%	-1.39%	-0.74%
1980s	3.81%	7.22%	11.67%	8.54%	8.50%
1990s	1.95%	4.87%	14.71%	6.61%	5.27%
2000s	0.19%	3.92%	-3.38%	4.19%	4.40%
2010s	-1.82%	2.17%	13.73%	6.02%	4.85%
Volatility	2.38%	4.33%	9.78%	3.79%	3.32%

Source: Global Financial Data

MORE BACKGROUND READING

Diversification and Risk Management, Balancing Betas, Counter-Point to Risk Parity Critiques
First Quadrant, http://www.firstquadrant.com/

"At Par with Risk Parity?"
Kunz, Policemen's Fund of Chicago,
http://www.cfainstitute.org/learning/products/publications/cp/Pages/cp.v28.n3.6.aspx

"I Want to Break Free, The Hidden Risks of Risk Parity Portfolio's
GMO, http://www.gmo.com

"Risk Parity—In the Spotlight after 50 Years"
NEPC
http://www.nepc.com/writable/research_articles/file/2010_03_nepc_risk_parity.pdf

"Leverage Aversion and Risk Parity", "Chasing Your Own Tail (Risk)"
AQR, http://www.econ.yale.edu/~af227/pdf/Leverage%20Aversion%20and%20
Risk%20Parity%20-%20Asness%20,%20Frazzini%20and%20Pedersen.pdf

"The Biggest Mistake in Investing", Engineering Targeted Returns and Risks"
Bridgewater, http://www.bwater.com/

"Risk Parity White Paper"
Meketa, http://www.meketagroup.com/documents/RiskParityWP_001.pdf

"On the Properties of Equally-Weighted Risk Contributions Portfolios"
Maillard et al., http://papers.ssrn.com/sol3/papers.cfm?abstract_id=1271972

"Demystifying Equity Risk-Based Strategies: A Simple Alpha plus Beta Description"
Carvalho et al., http://papers.ssrn.com/sol3/papers.cfm?abstract_id=1949003

"Risk Parity Portfolios™: The Next Generation", "PanAgora risk parity"
PanAgora
https://www.panagora.com/assets/PanAgora-Risk-Parity-The-Next-Generation.pdf

"The Risk Parity Approach to Asset Allocation"
Callan, http://www.top1000funds.com/attachments/TheRiskParityApproachtoAs-setAllocation2010.pdf

"Risk Parity for the Masses"
Steiner, http://papers.ssrn.com/sol3/papers.cfm?abstract_id=1955906

"Risk Parity in a Rising Rates Regime"
Salient, http://ww2.plansponsor.com/events/invites/SalientWhitepaper-RiskPar-ityinaRisingRatesRegime.pdf

CHAPTER 5

THE PERMANENT PORTFOLIO

Harry Browne was an author of over 12 books, a one-time Presidential candidate, and a financial advisor. The basic portfolio that he designed in the 1980s was balanced across four simple assets, and you can see Harry explain the theory here:[1]

"For the money you need to take care of you for the rest of your life, set up a simple, balanced, diversified portfolio. I call this a "Permanent Portfolio" because once you set it up, you never need to rearrange the investment mix—even if your outlook for the future changes. The portfolio should assure that your wealth will survive any event—including an event that would be devastating to any individual element within the portfolio... It isn't difficult or complicated to have such a portfolio this safe. You can achieve a great deal of diversification with a surprisingly simple portfolio."

Although the portfolio underperformed stocks, it was incredibly consistent across all market environments with low volatility and drawdowns. This presents a classic dilemma for investors,

---

1   crawlingroad.com/blog/2008/12/17/the-permanent-portfolio-and-the-16-golden-rules-of-financial-safety

particularly professional advisors. What is the trade-off for being different? Despite the incredibly consistent performance there are many years this portfolio would have underperformed U.S. stocks or a 60/40 allocation. Can you survive those periods even if you believe this portfolio to be superior? See FIGURE 28.

NOMINAL RETURNS 1973-2013

	T-BILLS	BONDS	STOCKS	PERMANENT
Returns	5.27%	7.74%	10.21%	8.53%
Volatility	0.97%	8.43%	15.57%	7.29%
Sharpe	0.00	0.29	0.32	0.45
Max Drawdown	0.00%	-15.79%	-50.95%	-12.74%

REAL RETURNS 1973-2013

	T-BILLS	BONDS	STOCKS	PERMANENT
Returns	0.99%	3.34%	5.71%	4.12%
Volatility	1.24%	8.73%	15.74%	7.48%
Sharpe	0.00	0.27	0.30	0.42
Max Drawdown	0.00%	-44.75%	-54.12%	-23.62%

REAL RETURNS 1973-1981

	T-BILLS	BONDS	STOCKS	PERMANENT
Returns	-0.71%	-5.08%	-3.92%	0.92%

REAL RETURNS 1982-2013

	T-BILLS	BONDS	STOCKS	PERMANENT
Returns	1.48%	5.85%	8.61%	5.05%

REAL RETURNS 1973-2013

	T-BILLS	BONDS	STOCKS	PERMANENT
1970s	-1.55%	-4.23%	-5.26%	3.20%
1980s	3.81%	7.22%	11.67%	4.61%
1990s	1.95%	4.87%	14.71%	4.12%
2000s	0.19%	3.92%	-3.38%	3.91%
2010s	-1.82%	2.17%	13.73%	4.80%
Volatility	2.38%	4.33%	9.78%	0.63%

US Large Cap	Stocks	8%
US Small Cap	Stocks	
Foreign Developed	Stocks	8%
Foreign Emerging	Stocks	
Corporate Bonds	Stocks/Bonds	35%
T-Bills	Bonds	
10 Year Bonds	Bonds	35%
30 Year Bonds	Bonds	
10 Year Foreign Bonds	Bonds	
TIPS	Real Assets	
Commodities	Real Assets	5%
Gold	Real Assets	5%
REITs	Real Assets	5%

Source: Browne

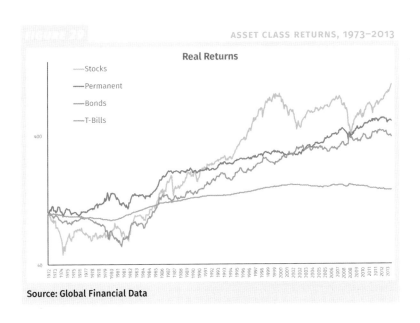

Real Returns

—Stocks
—Permanent
—Bonds
—T-Bills

Source: Global Financial Data

Next to Marc Faber's allocation that we profile later in the book, this allocation has the highest weighting to gold. Gold is an emotional topic for investors, and usually they fall on one side or another with a very strong opinion for or against. We think you should learn to become asset class agnostic and appreciate each asset class for its unique characteristics. Gold had the highest real returns of any asset class in the inflationary 1970s but also the worst performance from 1982–2013. However, adding gold (and to a lesser extent other real assets like commodities and TIPS) could have helped protect the portfolio during a rising inflation environment. Gold also performs well in an environment of negative real interest rates—that is when inflation is higher than current bond yields.

The next portfolio we look at just aims to be average, and it turns out that isn't a bad thing.

CHAPTER 6

THE GLOBAL MARKET PORTFOLIO

"We have a passion for keeping things simple."

— CHARLIE MUNGER, VICE-CHAIRMAN

BERKSHIRE HATHAWAY

Why not just invest along the weightings of the global market cap weighted portfolio? The main difficulty is that it is hard to determine exactly what the exact weightings are, but a number of researchers have come pretty close with a ballpark estimate.

A paper titled "Strategic Asset Allocation: The Global Multi-Asset Market Portfolio 1959–2011"[1] breaks out the broad world market portfolio.

Credit Suisse also looks at the global portfolio[2], and FIGURE 30 breaks out their allocations. We simplify this to the following allocation (FIGURE 31), labeled "GMP" for Global Market Portfolio,

---

1   https://www.credit-suisse.com/us/en/news-and-expertise/research/cred-it-suisse-research-institute/publications.html
2   https://www.credit-suisse.com/us/en/news-and-expertise/research/cred-it-suisse-research-institute/publications.html

to see how this portfolio performed.

FIGURE 30   THE GLOBAL MARKET PORTFOLIO, ("GMP")

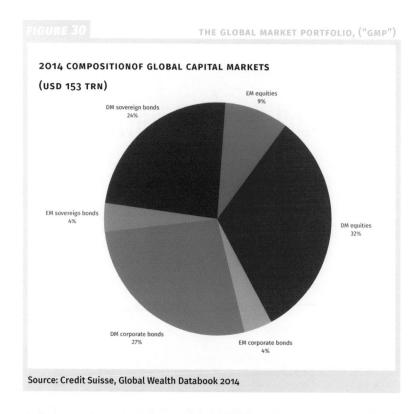

2014 COMPOSITIONOF GLOBAL CAPITAL MARKETS

(USD 153 TRN)

EM equities
9%

DM sovereign bonds
24%

DM equities
32%

EM sovereign bonds
4%

DM corporate bonds
27%

EM corporate bonds
4%

Source: Credit Suisse, Global Wealth Databook 2014

NOTE: THIS DOES NOT REFLECT THE EXACT GLOBAL MARKET PORTFOLIO OVER TIME SINCE IT IS ESTIMATED FROM TODAY'S WEIGHTINGS—BUT IT SHOULD BE A CLOSE APPROXIMATION. IT IS INTERESTING TO NOTE THAT THE TRUE GLOBAL MARKET PORTFOLIO WOULD NEVER REBALANCE—TALK ABOUT A LAZY PORTFOLIO.

US Large Cap	Stocks	20%
US Small Cap	Stocks	
Foreign Developed	Stocks	15%
Foreign Emerging	Stocks	5%
Corporate Bonds	Stocks/Bonds	22%
T-Bills	Bonds	
10 Year Bonds	Bonds	
30 Year Bonds	Bonds	15%
10 Year Foreign Bonds	Bonds	16%
TIPS	Real Assets	2%
Commodities	Real Assets	
Gold	Real Assets	
REITs	Real Assets	5%

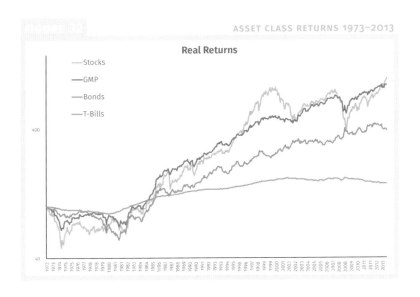

Real Returns

— Stocks
— GMP
— Bonds
— T-Bills

NOMINAL RETURNS 1973–2013

	T-BILLS	BONDS	STOCKS	GMP
Returns	5.27%	7.74%	10.21%	9.90%
Volatility	0.97%	8.43%	15.57%	8.45%
Sharpe	0.00	0.29	0.32	0.55
Max Drawdown	0.00%	-15.79%	-50.95%	-26.87%

REAL RETURNS 1973–2013

	T-BILLS	BONDS	STOCKS	GMP
Returns	0.99%	3.34%	5.71%	5.42%
Volatility	1.24%	8.73%	15.74%	8.76%
Sharpe	0.00	0.27	0.30	0.50
Max Drawdown	0.00%	-44.75%	-54.12%	-34.10%

REAL RETURNS 1973–1981

	T-BILLS	BONDS	STOCKS	GMP
Returns	-0.71%	-5.08%	-3.92%	-2.97%

REAL RETURNS 1982–2013

	T-BILLS	BONDS	STOCKS	GMP
Returns	1.48%	5.85%	8.61%	7.92%

REAL RETURNS 1973–2013

	T-BILLS	BONDS	STOCKS	GMP
1970s	-1.55%	-4.23%	-5.26%	-2.56%
1980s	3.81%	7.22%	11.67%	10.65%
1990s	1.95%	4.87%	14.71%	7.89%
2000s	0.19%	3.92%	-3.38%	3.13%
2010s	-1.82%	2.17%	13.73%	6.59%
Volatility	2.38%	4.33%	9.78%	5.08%

Source: Global Financial Data

We don't include commodities in this portfolio since it is difficult to estimate market composition, but we believe they provide
a vital portfolio diversification element. So what if you altered
the above global market portfolio to include commodities? In
this case, we're ball-parking a reasonable number, and we add
a 5% allocation each to commodities and gold, and reduce the
other allocations proportionally. We will call this portfolio the
Global Asset Allocation or "GAA" portfolio. The results were not
hugely different, though risk-adjusted returns did improve, as
did the consistency.

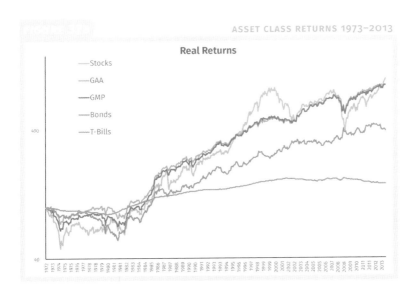

NOMINAL RETURNS 1973-2013

	T-BILLS	BONDS	STOCKS	GMP	GAA
Returns	5.27%	7.74%	10.21%	9.90%	9.90%
Volatility	0.97%	8.43%	15.57%	8.45%	7.99%
Sharpe	0.00	0.29	0.32	0.55	0.58
Max Drawdown	0.00%	-15.79%	-50.95%	-26.87%	-26.72%

REAL RETURNS 1973-2013

	T-BILLS	BONDS	STOCKS	GMP	GAA
Returns	0.99%	3.34%	5.71%	5.42%	5.43%
Volatility	1.24%	8.73%	15.74%	8.76%	8.25%
Sharpe	0.00	0.27	0.30	0.50	0.54
Max Drawdown	0.00%	-44.75%	-54.12%	-34.10%	-27.45%

REAL RETURNS 1973-1981

	T-BILLS	BONDS	STOCKS	GMP	GAA
Returns	-0.71%	-5.08%	-3.92%	-2.97%	-1.55%

REAL RETURNS 1982-2013

	T-BILLS	BONDS	STOCKS	GMP	GAA
Returns	1.48%	5.85%	8.61%	7.92%	7.50%

REAL RETURNS 1973-2013

	T-BILLS	BONDS	STOCKS	GMP	GAA
1970s	-1.55%	-4.23%	-5.26%	-2.56%	-0.34%
1980s	3.81%	7.22%	11.67%	10.65%	9.57%
1990s	1.95%	4.87%	14.71%	7.89%	6.90%
2000s	0.19%	3.92%	-3.38%	3.13%	3.71%
2010s	-1.82%	2.17%	13.73%	6.59%	6.06%
Volatility	2.38%	4.33%	9.78%	5.08%	3.73%

Source: Global Financial Data

CHAPTER 7

THE ROB ARNOTT PORTFOLIO

Rob Arnott is the founder and chairman of Research Affiliates, a research firm that has over $170 billion in assets managed using its strategies. He published over 100 articles in financial journals, as well as having served as the editor of the Financial Analysts Journal. His book *The Fundamental Index: A Better Way to Invest* focuses on smart beta strategies.

Smart beta is a phrase that refers to strategies that move away from the broad market cap portfolio. (So in U.S. stocks, think the S&P 500 versus a portfolio sorted on dividends or perhaps equally weighted.) The market cap portfolio is the market, and the returns of the market portfolio are the returns the population of investors receive before fees, transaction costs, etc. However, market cap weighting is problematic.

Market cap weighted indexes have only one variable—size—which is largely determined by price. (While not the topic of this book, market cap indexes often overweight expensive markets and bubbles—you can find more information in our book *Global Value*.) Many smart beta strategies weight their holdings by factors that have long shown outperformance, including value, momentum, quality, carry, and volatility. Here is a fun interview with William Bernstein[1] on portfolio tilts. We are big proponents of smart beta and factor tilts applied to a portfolio.

To the right is one sample allocation from an article Mr. Arnott authored in 2008. Another solid performer! To be fair, there is a zero chance that he would have used market cap weighted allocations in his portfolio, but we're trying to compare apples to apples for now. We examine one smart beta portfolio in the appendix.

1   http://www.etf.com/sections/features/19168-william-bernstein-be-open-to-new-factor-tilts.html

US Large Cap	Stocks	10%
US Small Cap	Stocks	
Foreign Developed	Stocks	10%
Foreign Emerging	Stocks	
Corporate Bonds	Stocks/Bonds	20%
T-Bills	Bonds	
10 Year Bonds	Bonds	
30 Year Bonds	Bonds	10%
10 Year Foreign Bonds	Bonds	20%
TIPS	Real Assets	10%
Commodities	Real Assets	10%
Gold	Real Assets	
REITs	Real Assets	10%

Source: Liquid Alternatives: More than Hedge Funds, 2008

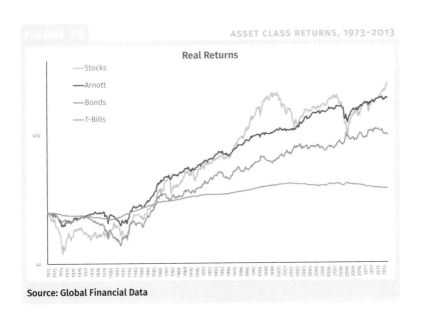

ASSET CLASS RETURNS, 1973–2013

Real Returns

— Stocks
— Arnott
— Bonds
— T-Bills

Source: Global Financial Data

	T-BILLS	BONDS	STOCKS	ARNOTT
Returns	5.27%	7.74%	10.21%	9.50%
Volatility	0.97%	8.43%	15.57%	7.19%
Sharpe	0.00	0.29	0.32	0.59
Max Drawdown	0.00%	-15.79%	-50.95%	-27.17%

REAL RETURNS 1973-2013

	T-BILLS	BONDS	STOCKS	ARNOTT
Returns	0.99%	3.34%	5.71%	5.04%
Volatility	1.24%	8.73%	15.74%	7.44%
Sharpe	0.00	0.27	0.30	0.54
Max Drawdown	0.00%	-44.75%	-54.12%	-25.96%

REAL RETURNS 1973-1981

	T-BILLS	BONDS	STOCKS	ARNOTT
Returns	-0.71%	-5.08%	-3.92%	-1.88%

REAL RETURNS 1982-2013

	T-BILLS	BONDS	STOCKS	ARNOTT
Returns	1.48%	5.85%	8.61%	7.28%

REAL RETURNS 1973-2013

	T-BILLS	BONDS	STOCKS	ARNOTT
1970s	-1.55%	-4.23%	-5.26%	-0.81%
1980s	3.81%	7.22%	11.67%	8.86%
1990s	1.95%	4.87%	14.71%	9.78%
2000s	0.19%	3.92%	-3.38%	0.34%
2010s	-1.82%	2.17%	13.73%	7.91%
Volatility	2.38%	4.33%	9.78%	5.04%

Source: Global Financial Data

CHAPTER 8

THE MARC FABER PORTFOLIO

Marc Faber is a Swiss economist and fund manager, living in Asia, who writes the Gloom, Boom, and Doom[1] market newsletter. And before you ask, no we're not directly related—although my father's side is from Germany and France and so there is a chance we have some shared blood somewhere.) While he often contributes long and short investment ideas to the Barron's Roundtable, he has stated numerous times his rough asset allocation is 25% each in gold, stocks, bonds and cash, and real estate. Marc probably holds some bonds and real estate in foreign markets, but the simple portfolio will do for a general discussion. While he doesn't explicitly say that he would split his stocks into U.S. and foreign, we assume that to be the case.

This was a surprise to me, but Marc's simple allocation is one of the most consistent we have reviewed. The portfolio is one of the few that had positive real returns in each decade. FIGURE 35 displays the Marc Faber Portfolio.

1   http://www.gloomboomdoom.com/

FIGURE 35   MARC FABER PORTFOLIO

US Large Cap	Stocks	13%
US Small Cap	Stocks	
Foreign Developed	Stocks	8%
Foreign Emerging	Stocks	4%
Corporate Bonds	Stocks/Bonds	
T-Bills	Bonds	
10 Year Bonds	Bonds	25%
30 Year Bonds	Bonds	
10 Year Foreign Bonds	Bonds	
TIPS	Real Assets	
Commodities	Real Assets	
Gold	Real Assets	25%
REITs	Real Assets	25%

Source: CNBC

FIGURE 36   ASSET CLASS RETURNS, 1973–2013

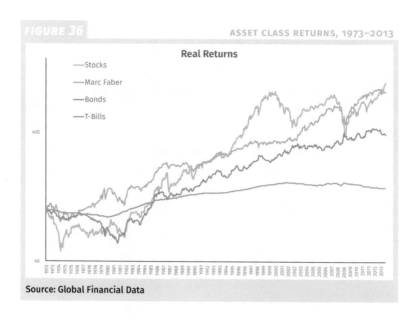

Real Returns

— Stocks
— Marc Faber
— Bonds
— T-Bills

Source: Global Financial Data

	T-BILLS	BONDS	STOCKS	MARC FABER
Returns	5.27%	7.74%	10.21%	9.72%
Volatility	0.97%	8.43%	15.57%	9.73%
Sharpe	0.00	0.29	0.32	0.46
Max Drawdown	0.00%	-15.79%	-50.95%	-28.14%

REAL RETURNS 1973-2013

	T-BILLS	BONDS	STOCKS	MARC FABER
Returns	0.99%	3.34%	5.71%	5.26%
Volatility	1.24%	8.73%	15.74%	9.86%
Sharpe	0.00	0.27	0.30	0.43
Max Drawdown	0.00%	-44.75%	-54.12%	-28.70%

REAL RETURNS 1973-1981

	T-BILLS	BONDS	STOCKS	MARC FABER
Returns	-0.71%	-5.08%	-3.92%	2.25%

REAL RETURNS 1982-2013

	T-BILLS	BONDS	STOCKS	MARC FABER
Returns	1.48%	5.85%	8.61%	6.49%

REAL RETURNS 1973-2013

	T-BILLS	BONDS	STOCKS	MARC FABER
1970s	-1.55%	-4.23%	-5.26%	4.37%
1980s	3.81%	7.22%	11.67%	5.62%
1990s	1.95%	4.87%	14.71%	8.36%
2000s	0.19%	3.92%	-3.38%	3.58%
2010s	-1.82%	2.17%	13.73%	4.98%
Volatility	2.38%	4.33%	9.78%	1.83%

Source: Global Financial Data

CHAPTER 9

THE ENDOWMENT PORTFOLIO: SWENSEN, EL-ERIAN, AND IVY

"Because for any given level of return, if you diversify, you can generate that return with a lower risk; or for any given level of risk, if you diversify, you can generate a higher return. So it's a free lunch. Diversification makes your portfolio better."

— DAVID SWENSEN, CIO YALE ENDOWMENT

We're not going to spend too much time describing the endowment style of investing—after all, it was the topic of our book in 2009—*The Ivy Portfolio*. The hallmarks of the endowment approach are a large allocation to equity-like assets, a global focus, a long time horizon, and active management where it can add value. While the endowment portfolios are much more complicated and illiquid than our 13 asset classes can cover due mainly to private equity and hedge fund allocations, the managers of the two largest endowments (Harvard and Yale) have, in their books over the years, proposed allocations for individual investors.

David Swensen, CIO for the Yale endowment, mentioned an allocation recommendation for individuals in his book *Unconventional Success* in 2005. Former Harvard endowment manager (and former PIMCO co-CIO) Mohamad El-Erian also published an allocation in his 2008 book *When Markets Collide*. For some odd reason El-Erian's allocation didn't add up to 100%, and a few categories like "special situations" are not directly investable in. We made some basic assumptions but the overall portfolio targets should be nearly the same.

We proposed a more basic version in *The Ivy Portfolio* that was meant to replicate the broad endowment space. While these three basic allocations are solid performers, they underperform the *actual* top endowments like Harvard and Yale by about 3–4 percentage points per annum. There are several reasons why (private equity allocation, leverage, factor tilts, possible alpha generation from the managers), and a number of researchers have examined the endowments at length. One such article is by Peter Mladina titled "Yale's Endowment Returns: Manager Skill or Risk Exposure?"[1] Here we examine how these three allocations have performed over time.

1   http://www.iijournals.com/doi/abs/10.3905/JWM.2010.13.1.043

		IVY	EL-ERIAN	SWENSEN
US Large Cap	Stocks	20%	18%	20%
US Small Cap	Stocks			
Foreign Developed	Stocks	20%	18%	20%
Foreign Emerging	Stocks		15%	10%
Corporate Bonds	Stocks/Bonds			
T-Bills	Bonds			
10 Year Bonds	Bonds	20%		
30 Year Bonds	Bonds		6%	15%
10 Year Foreign Bonds	Bonds		11%	
TIPS	Real Assets		6%	15%
Commodities	Real Assets	20%	13%	
Gold	Real Assets			
REITs	Real Assets	20%	13%	20%

Source: Unconventional Success, 2005, When Markets Collide, 2008, Ivy Portfolio, 2009

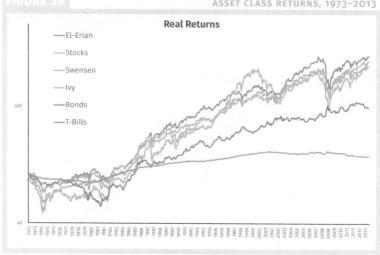

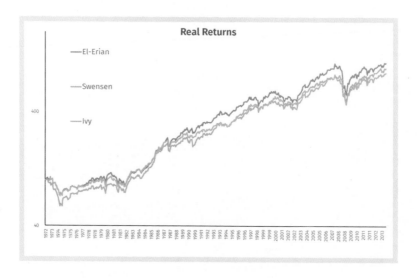

	T-BILLS	BONDS	STOCKS	IVY	EL-ERIAN	SWENSEN
Returns	5.27%	7.74%	10.21%	9.90%	10.45%	10.16%
Volatility	0.97%	8.43%	15.57%	10.21%	10.69%	10.68%
Sharpe	0.00	0.29	0.32	0.45	0.48	0.46
Max Drawdown	0.00%	-15.79%	-50.95%	-46.00%	-45.72%	-41.60%

REAL RETURNS 1973-2013

	T-BILLS	BONDS	STOCKS	IVY	EL-ERIAN	SWENSEN
Returns	0.99%	3.34%	5.71%	5.44%	5.96%	5.67%
Volatility	1.24%	8.73%	15.74%	10.35%	10.83%	10.92%
Sharpe	0.00	0.27	0.30	0.43	0.46	0.43
Max Drawdown	0.00%	-44.75%	-54.12%	-45.50%	-46.47%	-42.51%

REAL RETURNS 1973-1981

	T-BILLS	BONDS	STOCKS	IVY	EL-ERIAN	SWENSEN
Returns	-0.71%	-5.08%	-3.92%	-0.82%	-0.05%	-1.66%

REAL RETURNS 1982-2013

	T-BILLS	BONDS	STOCKS	IVY	EL-ERIAN	SWENSEN
Returns	1.48%	5.85%	8.61%	7.29%	7.74%	7.85%

REAL RETURNS 1973-2013

	T-BILLS	BONDS	STOCKS	IVY	EL-ERIAN	SWENSEN
1970s	-1.55%	-4.23%	-5.26%	-0.18%	0.58%	-2.20%
1980s	3.81%	7.22%	11.67%	10.13%	10.62%	10.74%
1990s	1.95%	4.87%	14.71%	6.54%	7.39%	7.36%
2000s	0.19%	3.92%	-3.38%	2.99%	3.66%	3.69%
2010s	-1.82%	2.17%	13.73%	7.26%	6.20%	8.16%
Volatility	2.38%	4.33%	9.78%	4.00%	3.80%	5.01%

Source: Global Financial Data

CHAPTER 10

THE WARREN BUFFETT ASSET ALLOCATION PORTFOLIO

Warren Buffett mentioned asset allocation instructions for his trust in his 2013 shareholder letter:[1]

"What I advise here is essentially identical to certain instructions I've laid out in my will. One bequest provides that cash will be delivered to a trustee for my wife's benefit. ... My advice to the trustee could not be more simple: Put 10% of the cash in short-term government bonds and 90% in a very low-cost S&P 500 index fund. (I suggest Vanguard's.) I believe the trust's long-term results from this policy will be superior to those attained by most investors ..."

How has that advice performed over time? You don't need us to tell you, but with 90% in stocks, you're going to track the broad stock market.

---

1   http://www.berkshirehathaway.com/letters/2013ltr.pdf

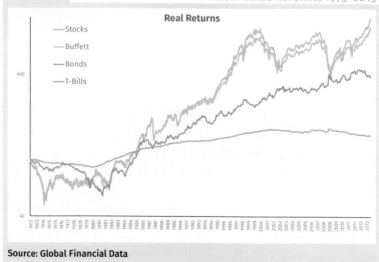

Source: Global Financial Data

	T-BILLS	BONDS	STOCKS	BUFFETT
Returns	5.27%	7.74%	10.21%	9.82%
Volatility	0.97%	8.43%	15.57%	14.01%
Sharpe	0.00	0.29	0.32	0.32
Max Drawdown	0.00%	-15.79%	-50.95%	-47.02%

REAL RETURNS 1973-2013

	T-BILLS	BONDS	STOCKS	BUFFETT
Returns	0.99%	3.34%	5.71%	5.35%
Volatility	1.24%	8.73%	15.74%	14.19%
Sharpe	0.00	0.27	0.30	0.31
Max Drawdown	0.00%	-44.75%	-54.12%	-49.78%

REAL RETURNS 1973-1981

	T-BILLS	BONDS	STOCKS	BUFFETT
Returns	-0.71%	-5.08%	-3.92%	-3.48%

REAL RETURNS 1982-2013

	T-BILLS	BONDS	STOCKS	BUFFETT
Returns	1.48%	5.85%	8.61%	7.99%

REAL RETURNS 1973-2013

	T-BILLS	BONDS	STOCKS	BUFFETT
1970s	-1.55%	-4.23%	-5.26%	-4.78%
1980s	3.81%	7.22%	11.67%	11.00%
1990s	1.95%	4.87%	14.71%	13.47%
2000s	0.19%	3.92%	-3.38%	-2.91%
2010s	-1.82%	2.17%	13.73%	12.17%
Volatility	2.38%	4.33%	9.78%	8.86%

Source: Global Financial Data

CHAPTER 11

COMPARISON OF THE STRATEGIES

"I believe in the discipline of mastering the best that other people have ever figured out. I don't believe in just sitting there and trying to dream it up all yourself. Nobody's that smart."

— CHARLIE MUNGER

The funny thing about all the various iterations of our 13 asset class building blocks is that you can basically simplify them into three broad categories: stocks, bonds, and real assets. We selected one allocation from each chapter for a comparison (otherwise it wouldn't fit on one page). The criteria wasn't that sophisticated—we just tried to pick the most heralded allocation from each chapter.

Once you do simplify the exposures, you can see in FIGURE 40 that many of the allocations have fairly similar broad exposures. The exceptions are 60/40 and the Buffett allocations since they place zero in real assets.

FIGURE 40

ASSET CLASS BROAD ALLOCATION

	ALL SEASONS	PERMANENT	GAA	60/40	ARNOTT	MARC FABER	EL-ERIAN	BUFFET
Stocks	30%	25%	46%	60%	30%	25%	51%	90%
Bonds	55%	50%	38%	40%	40%	25%	17%	10%
Real Assets	15%	25%	16%		30%	50%	32%	

Note that many of the allocations were recommended to the public at different times over the years, and the later recommendations possibly benefitted from knowledge of past returns. However, as we show below, it really doesn't matter that much!

ASSET CLASS NOMINAL RETURNS, 1973-2013

	T-BILLS	BONDS	STOCKS	ALL SEASONS	PERMANE
Returns	5.27%	7.74%	10.21%	9.50%	8.53%
Volatility	0.97%	8.43%	15.57%	8.24%	7.29%
Sharpe	0.00	0.29	0.32	0.51	0.45
Max Drawdown	0.00%	-15.79%	-50.95%	-14.59%	-12.74%

ASSET CLASS REAL RETURNS, 1973-2013

Returns	0.99%	3.34%	5.71%	5.04%	4.12%
Volatility	1.24%	8.73%	15.74%	8.56%	7.48%
Sharpe	0.00	0.27	0.30	0.47	0.42
Max Drawdown	0.00%	-44.75%	-54.12%	-28.77%	-23.62%

ASSET CLASS RETURNS, 1973-2013

1973-1981	-0.71%	-5.08%	-3.92%	-2.83%	0.92%
1982-2013	1.48%	5.85%	8.61%	7.38%	5.05%
1970s	-1.55%	-4.23%	-5.26%	-1.39%	3.20%
1980s	3.81%	7.22%	11.67%	8.54%	4.61%
1990s	1.95%	4.87%	14.71%	6.61%	4.12%
2000s	0.19%	3.92%	-3.38%	4.19%	3.91%
2010s	-1.82%	2.17%	13.73%	6.02%	4.80%
Volatility	2.38%	4.33%	9.78%	3.79%	0.63%

GAA	60/40	ARNOTT	MARC FABER	EL-ERIAN	BUFFETT
9.90%	9.60%	9.50%	9.72%	10.45%	9.82%
7.99%	10.20%	7.19%	9.73%	10.69%	14.01%
0.58	0.42	0.59	0.46	0.48	0.32
-26.72%	-29.28%	-27.17%	-28.14%	-45.72%	-47.02%
5.43%	5.13%	5.04%	5.26%	5.96%	5.35%
8.25%	10.46%	7.44%	9.86%	10.83%	14.19%
0.54	0.39	0.54	0.43	0.46	0.31
-27.45%	-39.35%	-25.96%	-28.70%	-46.47%	-49.78%
-1.55%	-4.05%	-1.88%	2.25%	-0.05%	-3.48%
7.50%	7.88%	7.09%	6.14%	7.74%	7.99%
-0.34%	-4.56%	-0.81%	4.37%	0.58%	-4.78%
9.57%	10.28%	8.86%	5.62%	10.62%	11.00%
6.90%	10.89%	6.20%	3.71%	7.39%	13.47%
3.71%	-0.04%	4.17%	6.41%	3.66%	-2.91%
6.06%	9.44%	5.25%	6.66%	6.20%	12.17%
3.73%	7.05%	3.56%	1.28%	3.80%	8.86%

Most of the allocations moved together in a similar fashion. However, the allocations that performed the best in the inflationary 1970s then turned around and performed the worst in the disinflationary period to follow. Also not surprisingly, the Buffett and 60/40 allocations, with a lack of real assets, performed the worst during the inflationary 1970s. Even with the difference in allocations, the spread between the worst-performing allocation, the Permanent Portfolio at 4.12%, and the best, the El-Erian Portfolio at 5.67%, was only 1.84%. That is astonishing. If you exclude the Permanent Portfolio, **all of the allocations are within one percentage point**.

And just in case there are readers that want to see the year-by-year nominal and real returns, here they are.

FIGURE 42A

ASSET CLASS NOMINAL RETURNS, 1973–2013

Source: Global Financial Data

	T-BILLS	BONDS	STOCKS
1973	7.29%	3.33%	-14.79%
1974	7.99%	4.09%	-26.54%
1975	5.87%	5.62%	37.25%
1976	5.07%	15.25%	23.70%
1977	5.45%	0.66%	-7.41%
1978	7.64%	-0.77%	6.44%
1979	10.56%	1.92%	18.35%
1980	12.10%	-1.07%	32.27%
1981	14.60%	5.55%	-5.05%
1982	10.94%	39.31%	21.48%
1983	8.99%	2.64%	22.50%
1984	9.90%	15.01%	6.15%
1985	7.71%	29.62%	31.65%
1986	6.09%	21.29%	18.60%
1987	5.88%	-2.22%	5.17%
1988	6.94%	7.02%	16.61%
1989	8.44%	17.79%	31.69%
1990	7.69%	7.88%	-3.10%
1991	5.43%	18.75%	30.47%
1992	3.48%	7.45%	7.62%
1993	3.03%	13.00%	10.08%
1994	4.39%	-7.32%	1.32%
1995	5.61%	25.94%	37.58%
1996	5.14%	0.13%	22.96%
1997	5.19%	12.02%	33.36%
1998	4.86%	14.45%	28.58%
1999	4.80%	-7.51%	21.04%
2000	5.98%	17.22%	-9.10%
2001	3.33%	5.53%	-11.89%
2002	1.61%	15.37%	-22.10%
2003	1.03%	0.46%	28.68%
2004	1.43%	4.61%	10.88%
2005	3.30%	3.09%	4.91%
2006	4.97%	2.21%	15.80%
2007	4.52%	10.54%	5.49%
2008	1.24%	20.23%	-37.00%
2009	0.15%	-9.50%	26.46%
2010	0.14%	7.26%	15.06%
2011	0.06%	16.71%	2.11%
2012	0.08%	2.77%	16.00%
2013	0.05%	-8.56%	32.39%

ALL SEASONS	PERMANENT	GAA	60/40	ARNOTT	MARC FABER	EL-ERIAN	BUFFETT
0.88%	11.27%	-5.88%	-7.65%	1.18%	6.92%	1.02%	-19.89%
-1.41%	8.63%	-11.62%	-14.95%	-4.34%	-3.92%	-11.70%	-32.13%
9.99%	4.85%	20.92%	24.10%	15.69%	11.83%	19.93%	25.34%
14.52%	10.99%	18.48%	20.51%	16.28%	18.70%	14.57%	16.17%
4.48%	5.83%	8.18%	-4.20%	9.67%	12.13%	11.91%	-12.11%
8.65%	13.02%	9.10%	3.75%	9.43%	13.44%	15.46%	-2.19%
15.21%	33.96%	7.21%	11.63%	9.31%	40.80%	19.02%	3.86%
9.39%	14.11%	12.75%	18.70%	10.31%	18.34%	21.42%	15.82%
-4.24%	-6.49%	-0.19%	-0.79%	-0.55%	-6.33%	-3.37%	-11.23%
29.58%	23.07%	23.78%	28.69%	26.37%	22.10%	10.60%	16.05%
6.95%	3.98%	14.45%	14.29%	13.03%	8.88%	18.36%	16.75%
9.33%	2.63%	12.26%	9.88%	11.28%	3.92%	9.43%	2.55%
31.16%	20.52%	32.62%	30.99%	26.34%	20.00%	27.38%	24.48%
25.88%	20.28%	28.32%	19.98%	23.25%	24.60%	24.38%	16.12%
4.28%	7.04%	9.39%	3.71%	9.05%	6.03%	13.92%	1.26%
11.93%	3.99%	15.78%	12.73%	14.08%	6.32%	21.08%	10.80%
23.01%	14.72%	18.29%	26.17%	14.75%	10.78%	23.87%	23.61%
3.25%	2.49%	-0.08%	1.35%	5.19%	-5.31%	-1.51%	-7.75%
18.39%	10.69%	22.59%	25.92%	17.40%	17.48%	23.68%	24.09%
5.78%	3.20%	6.49%	7.63%	6.85%	3.80%	4.91%	4.19%
17.11%	13.30%	19.48%	11.29%	12.82%	19.43%	21.87%	6.46%
-4.63%	-1.75%	-1.89%	-2.16%	-1.35%	-1.45%	0.40%	-0.99%
27.09%	16.96%	23.60%	32.88%	22.38%	14.48%	18.10%	30.78%
6.03%	4.99%	10.25%	13.42%	13.14%	10.80%	16.26%	17.29%
12.13%	7.31%	12.87%	24.65%	8.71%	5.22%	6.57%	28.23%
12.41%	13.24%	14.77%	23.64%	6.12%	2.58%	-0.21%	24.29%
3.73%	3.08%	6.36%	8.96%	4.32%	3.59%	19.97%	16.30%
10.25%	3.19%	1.78%	0.93%	11.31%	5.20%	1.92%	-10.61%
-2.54%	0.29%	-1.02%	-4.55%	-1.44%	2.73%	-7.62%	-11.75%
6.14%	3.89%	0.10%	-7.86%	7.96%	6.42%	-0.01%	-21.73%
14.11%	12.69%	21.61%	16.96%	19.50%	23.37%	31.18%	23.31%
11.59%	7.41%	13.25%	8.46%	13.87%	14.28%	18.83%	6.46%
11.43%	9.43%	5.60%	4.32%	5.11%	10.72%	12.86%	1.24%
6.79%	11.15%	12.24%	10.23%	8.00%	20.37%	15.30%	11.81%
13.93%	12.92%	8.77%	7.73%	8.62%	8.24%	12.98%	1.31%
-0.24%	0.55%	-15.32%	-17.46%	-14.25%	-15.03%	-32.68%	-33.72%
-0.87%	5.42%	15.73%	11.28%	13.69%	20.87%	26.80%	20.49%
12.79%	13.49%	9.31%	12.74%	8.29%	20.08%	12.35%	12.01%
16.72%	12.49%	6.92%	8.26%	8.23%	7.86%	0.12%	-0.96%
7.29%	6.64%	12.28%	10.81%	10.38%	11.99%	13.26%	12.47%
-3.47%	-4.41%	6.15%	14.44%	2.36%	-3.72%	7.73%	26.91%

	T-BILLS	BONDS	STOCKS
1973	-1.33%	-4.97%	-21.82%
1974	-3.91%	-7.42%	-34.92%
1975	-1.01%	-1.25%	28.46%
1976	0.19%	9.93%	17.99%
1977	-1.18%	-5.69%	-13.29%
1978	-1.28%	-9.06%	-2.42%
1979	-2.44%	-10.13%	4.50%
1980	-0.38%	-12.21%	17.57%
1981	5.24%	-3.21%	-12.97%
1982	6.85%	34.20%	16.93%
1983	5.02%	-1.11%	18.09%
1984	5.74%	10.68%	2.11%
1985	3.78%	24.96%	26.92%
1986	4.93%	19.92%	17.26%
1987	1.38%	-6.42%	0.74%
1988	2.42%	2.50%	11.72%
1989	3.63%	12.62%	25.95%
1990	1.49%	1.62%	-8.87%
1991	2.30%	15.26%	26.62%
1992	0.56%	4.42%	4.58%
1993	0.27%	10.01%	7.16%
1994	1.67%	-9.77%	-1.33%
1995	2.99%	22.88%	34.24%
1996	1.76%	-3.10%	19.08%
1997	3.43%	10.15%	31.15%
1998	3.20%	12.65%	26.57%
1999	2.06%	-9.94%	17.90%
2000	2.51%	13.42%	-12.08%
2001	1.74%	3.91%	-13.30%
2002	-0.76%	12.70%	-23.94%
2003	-0.85%	-1.40%	26.23%
2004	-1.78%	1.30%	7.39%
2005	-0.14%	-0.40%	1.37%
2006	2.35%	-0.39%	12.90%
2007	0.41%	6.21%	1.37%
2008	1.06%	19.75%	-36.96%
2009	-2.52%	-11.93%	23.04%
2010	-1.34%	5.68%	13.39%
2011	-2.84%	13.38%	-0.86%
2012	-1.65%	0.97%	14.09%
2013	-1.44%	-9.93%	30.44%

FIGURE 42B

ASSET CLASS REAL RETURNS,
1973–2013

Source: Global Financial Data

ALL SEASONS	PERMANENT	GAA	60/40	ARNOTT	MARC FABER	EL-ERIAN	BUFFETT
-7.32%	2.30%	-13.56%	-15.18%	-7.02%	-1.74%	-7.21%	-12.71%
-12.38%	-3.35%	-21.53%	-24.52%	-15.00%	-14.60%	-21.61%	-23.44%
2.87%	-1.96%	13.13%	16.11%	8.21%	4.57%	12.19%	33.93%
9.22%	5.85%	13.01%	14.95%	10.91%	13.22%	9.26%	21.80%
-2.10%	-0.82%	1.39%	-10.26%	2.79%	5.12%	4.90%	-6.15%
-0.35%	3.69%	0.07%	-4.90%	0.37%	4.08%	5.95%	6.68%
1.71%	18.45%	-5.43%	-1.49%	-3.55%	24.57%	5.11%	17.64%
-2.85%	1.39%	0.15%	5.46%	-2.04%	5.15%	7.91%	30.29%
-12.23%	-14.29%	-8.49%	-9.04%	-8.81%	-14.16%	-11.42%	-3.17%
24.76%	18.50%	19.16%	23.92%	21.68%	17.54%	6.43%	20.56%
3.05%	0.18%	10.29%	10.15%	8.92%	4.92%	14.07%	21.12%
5.19%	-1.27%	8.02%	5.72%	7.07%	-0.03%	5.28%	6.60%
26.44%	16.16%	27.86%	26.28%	21.79%	15.66%	22.79%	29.12%
24.46%	18.96%	26.87%	18.62%	21.86%	23.23%	22.97%	17.45%
-0.16%	2.50%	4.77%	-0.68%	4.43%	1.53%	9.12%	5.72%
7.22%	-0.42%	10.92%	7.99%	9.28%	1.82%	16.00%	15.65%
17.62%	9.66%	13.09%	20.66%	9.69%	5.88%	18.44%	29.25%
-2.77%	-3.48%	-5.95%	-4.62%	-0.92%	-10.88%	-7.29%	-1.93%
14.89%	7.41%	18.99%	22.22%	13.94%	14.02%	20.04%	27.86%
2.79%	0.28%	3.48%	4.59%	3.83%	0.86%	1.94%	7.22%
14.02%	10.29%	16.33%	8.35%	9.83%	16.28%	18.66%	9.37%
-7.14%	-4.32%	-4.46%	-4.73%	-3.93%	-4.03%	-2.23%	1.67%
23.99%	14.10%	20.58%	29.65%	19.38%	11.66%	15.18%	34.04%
2.63%	1.62%	6.72%	9.80%	9.52%	7.26%	12.56%	21.12%
10.26%	5.51%	10.98%	22.57%	6.89%	3.45%	4.78%	30.40%
10.63%	11.46%	12.96%	21.71%	4.44%	0.96%	-1.80%	26.26%
1.03%	0.40%	3.60%	6.12%	1.61%	0.91%	16.88%	19.40%
6.67%	-0.18%	-1.54%	-2.36%	7.69%	1.76%	-1.41%	-7.58%
-4.08%	-1.27%	-2.58%	-6.05%	-2.98%	1.15%	-9.10%	-10.31%
3.67%	1.47%	-2.23%	-10.02%	5.46%	3.96%	-2.32%	-19.83%
11.97%	10.57%	19.33%	14.75%	17.28%	21.05%	28.71%	25.70%
8.08%	4.03%	9.68%	5.03%	10.30%	10.70%	15.12%	9.93%
7.69%	5.76%	2.05%	0.80%	1.60%	7.01%	9.10%	4.78%
4.11%	8.39%	9.43%	7.46%	5.32%	17.41%	12.45%	14.68%
9.47%	8.50%	4.51%	3.52%	4.36%	3.98%	8.57%	5.44%
-0.50%	0.30%	-15.45%	-17.58%	-14.29%	-15.07%	-32.58%	-33.74%
-3.55%	2.58%	12.63%	8.28%	10.65%	17.61%	23.39%	23.83%
11.13%	11.83%	7.71%	11.09%	6.70%	18.33%	10.71%	13.66%
13.39%	9.28%	3.84%	5.13%	5.12%	4.76%	-2.77%	2.01%
5.43%	4.82%	10.36%	8.94%	8.49%	10.10%	11.35%	14.37%
-4.92%	-5.85%	4.56%	12.74%	0.82%	-5.17%	6.11%	28.81%

Another way of visualizing the visualizing the benefits of a simple asset allocation is to generate what is called a periodic table of returns—an obvious nod to the Periodic Table of Elements. Here we construct a table of seven basic asset classes and the generic "GAA" asset allocation to prove a simple point. With a broad asset allocation you will never have the best returns of any asset class, but you will also never have the worst!

ASSET CLASS REAL RETURNS, 1973–2013

T-Bills	US Bonds	US Stocks	Foreign EAFE	GSCI	REITs	Gold		GAA

1973	1974	1975	1976	1977	1978	1979
61.83%	52.32%	28.46%	42.19%	15.84%	25.56%	110.11%
61.26%	24.25%	28.31%	17.99%	11.98%	23.42%	18.27%
-1.33%	-3.91%	27.57%	13.01%	11.67%	20.84%	15.37%
-4.97%	-7.42%	13.13%	9.93%	3.44%	0.07%	4.50%
-13.56%	-21.53%	-1.01%	0.19%	1.39%	-1.28%	-2.44%
-21.23%	-31.00%	-1.25%	-1.11%	-1.18%	-2.42%	-5.48%
-21.82%	-34.92%	-22.71%	-8.31%	-5.69%	-9.06%	-6.34%
-33.33%	-48.90%	-27.87%	-16.08%	-13.29%	-9.89%	-10.13%

1980	1981	1982	1983	1984	1985	1986	1987	1988	1989
17.57%	5.24%	34.20%	20.93%	10.68%	51.16%	67.99%	19.76%	23.21%	32.25%
13.74%	-0.39%	26.74%	20.12%	10.49%	27.86%	26.87%	18.62%	22.56%	25.95%
10.62%	-3.21%	19.16%	18.09%	8.02%	26.92%	21.61%	15.10%	11.72%	13.09%
0.15%	-8.49%	16.93%	12.01%	5.74%	24.96%	19.92%	4.77%	10.92%	12.62%
-0.38%	-9.31%	8.25%	10.29%	3.76%	6.00%	17.87%	1.38%	6.66%	5.86%
-1.43%	-12.97%	7.39%	5.02%	2.11%	3.78%	17.26%	0.74%	2.50%	3.63%
-1.66%	-29.48%	6.85%	-1.11%	-2.80%	2.99%	4.93%	-6.42%	2.42%	-6.14%
-12.21%	-38.58%	-4.70%	-17.51%	-23.26%	2.05%	0.91%	-14.52%	-19.32%	-6.20%

1990	1991	1992	1993	1994	1995	1996	1997	1998	1999
21.90%	31.74%	9.01%	29.48%	5.25%	34.24%	31.44%	31.15%	26.57%	37.37%
1.62%	26.62%	4.58%	16.33%	2.58%	22.88%	29.71%	16.88%	18.45%	24.03%
1.49%	18.99%	4.42%	15.44%	1.67%	20.58%	19.08%	10.08%	12.96%	17.90%
-5.95%	15.26%	3.48%	14.50%	-1.33%	17.30%	6.72%	10.15%	12.65%	3.60%
-7.88%	9.16%	1.47%	10.01%	-1.84%	15.39%	2.96%	3.43%	3.20%	2.06%
-8.87%	2.30%	0.56%	7.16%	-4.46%	8.77%	1.76%	0.32%	-1.86%	-2.73%
-22.27%	-8.99%	-8.89%	0.27%	-4.80%	2.99%	-3.10%	-15.51%	-20.14%	-8.92%
-27.85%	-13.07%	-14.40%	-14.69%	-9.77%	-8.25%	-7.70%	-22.82%	-36.80%	-9.94%

2000	2001	2002	2003	2004	2005	2006	2007	2008	2009
44.92%	13.73%	29.10%	37.53%	26.36%	21.51%	31.00%	27.43%	19.75%	28.88%
21.82%	3.91%	21.54%	35.88%	16.92%	14.15%	23.77%	25.82%	5.18%	23.87%
13.42%	1.74%	12.70%	26.23%	13.72%	10.23%	20.16%	7.31%	1.06%	23.04%
2.51%	0.87%	2.79%	19.33%	9.60%	4.64%	12.90%	6.21%	-15.45%	21.46%
-1.54%	-2.58%	-0.76%	18.48%	7.39%	2.05%	9.43%	4.51%	-36.96%	12.63%
-8.47%	-13.30%	-2.13%	17.37%	2.30%	1.37%	2.35%	1.37%	-36.98%	10.44%
-12.08%	-22.51%	-18.25%	-0.85%	1.30%	-0.14%	-0.39%	0.41%	-43.04%	-2.52%
-16.80%	-33.04%	-23.94%	-1.40%	-1.78%	-0.40%	-17.05%	-21.13%	-46.01%	-11.93%

2010	2011	2012	2013
27.66%	13.38%	18.13%	30.44%
25.76%	7.07%	15.92%	21.44%
13.39%	4.16%	14.09%	4.56%
7.71%	3.84%	10.56%	1.67%
7.40%	-0.86%	5.30%	-1.44%
6.63%	-2.84%	0.97%	-2.70%
5.68%	-4.01%	-1.62%	-9.93%
-1.34%	-14.32%	-1.65%	-29.15%

CHAPTER 12

IMPLEMENTATION (ETFS, FEES, TAXES, ADVISORS)

"You can't control the market, but you can control what you pay. You have to try to get yourself on automatic pilot so your emotions don't kill you."

— BURTON MALKIEL, AUTHOR OF A
RANDOM WALK DOWN WALL STREET

The most important principle for all investors is that they have a plan and process for investing in any environment, regardless of how improbable or unfathomable that may be. Are you prepared for all of the possible outcomes, such as declines of 50–100% in any one asset? Are you prepared for currency devaluations, but also massive rallies in stocks or bonds? Can you fathom a world with interest rates at 0.1%? What about at 10%?

Modern portfolio theory holds that there is a tradeoff for investing in assets—you get paid to assume risk. One of the biggest things you can do for your portfolio is to remove your emotional decision-making. Look at the below chart and notice when people were most excited about stocks and most depressed. The exact wrong times! Study after study has shown how bad people are at timing their investments.[1] (It's not just individuals— it happens to professionals as well.)

FIGURE 43   AAII SENTIMENT SURVEY

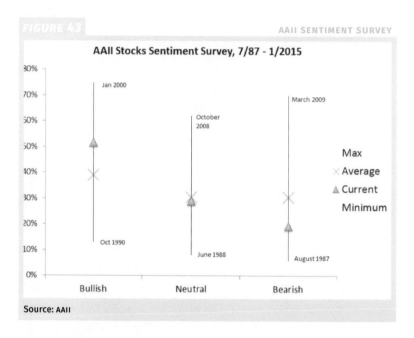

AAII Stocks Sentiment Survey, 7/87 - 1/2015

Source: AAII

Thus, first you need to get your emotions in check and have a plan. Then don't do dumb stuff when it gets hard. Easier to say than do, but very necessary.

REBALANCING

We said in our first book *The Ivy Portfolio* that rebalancing matters, as long as you do it *sometime*. The timeframe isn't all that important, and doing a yearly, or even every few year rebalance is just

---

1   http://blogs.wsj.com/moneybeat/2014/05/09/just-how-dumb-are-investors/

fine. Yearly is just nice since it lets you review your investments, as well as make tax optimal changes. If the accounts are taxable, tax harvesting the losses on a consistent basis can add to your after tax returns. Below is the global market portfolio (GMP) from earlier in the book rebalanced monthly and never, and you can see rebalancing or not the returns are quite similar, and differ by less than 0.50% per year. But 0.50% per year is worth rebalancing for! The nice thing about using an allocation ETF, mutual fund, or automated investment service is that the investment manager does the tax harvesting and rebalancing for you.

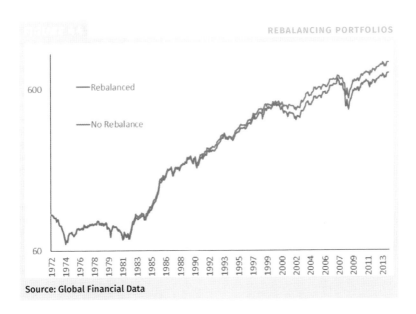

Source: Global Financial Data

FEES

Next, let's chat fees. Below are some ballpark fees for perspective:

- The average financial advisor charges 0.99% per year.

(Although the most expensive quarter of advisors charge over 2% per year.)

- The average ETF charges 0.57% per year.
- The average mutual fund charges 1.26% per year.

Source: PriceMetrix,[1] Morgan Stanley, 2013[2]

To let people know just how important fees are, below is an example.

What if you could predict the single best performing asset allocation ahead of time?

We took the best performing strategy, El-Erian, and compared it to the worst, the Permanent Portfolio. (Note we are just using real absolute returns and not risk adjusted where Permanent would rank much higher.)

What if someone was able to predict the best-performing strategy in 1973 and then decided to implement it via the average mutual fund? We also looked at the effect if someone decided to use a financial advisor who then invested client assets in the average mutual fund. Predicting the best asset allocation, but implementing it via the average mutual fund would push returns down to roughly even with the Permanent Portfolio. If you added advisory fees on top of that, it had the effect of transforming the **BEST** performing asset allocation into lower than the **WORST**. Think about that for a second. Fees are far more important than your asset allocation decision!

Now what do you spend most of your time thinking about? Probably the asset allocation decision and not fees! **This is the main point we are trying to drive home in this book—if you are going to allocate to a buy and hold portfolio you want to be paying as little as possible in total fees and costs.**

1   http://www.pricemetrix.com/
2   http://mebfaber.com/2013/06/05/mutual-fund-vs-etf-fees/

Source: Global Financial Data

There are many great advisors and brokers out there that charge reasonable fees. And many advisors offer value-added services, such as financial and estate planning and insurance. Vanguard estimates[3] the value of financial advisors can far outweigh the costs—mostly because they prevent you from doing even dumber things that you would do on your own.

However, if you are just looking for investment management services, you can simply buy a portfolio of ETFS, an asset allocation ETF or mutual fund, or enroll in any number of automated investment services (also called robo-advisors). There are a number of asset allocation ETFs that charge around and below 0.30% per year for a diversified global portfolio.

Below is a list of some automated services and their fees for a $100,000 portfolio. For comparison, here are a number of other famous investment advisors and their fees[4] —you may be sur-

3   http://www.vanguard.com/pdf/ISGQVAA.pdf
4   http://mebfaber.com/2014/10/29/fees-of-the-top-advisors/

prised you are paying your advisor up to and over 2% per year.

- Vanguard Personal Advisor Services[1] 0.30%
- Betterment[2] 0.15%
- WealthFront[3] 0.25%
- Liftoff[4] 0.40%
- AssetBuilder[5] 0.45%

Recall that for a $1 million portfolio, a 2% fee is $20,000 per year. Instead of it being automatically deducted from your account, imagine literally carrying a briefcase full of cash to your advisor each year—that may change your perspective!

TAXES

"One of the most serious problems in the mutual fund industry, which is full of serious problems, is that almost all mutual fund managers behave as if taxes don't matter. But taxes matter. Taxes matter a lot."

— DAVID SWENSEN

For a longer review on fees and taxes, take a look at "Rules of Prudence for Individual Investors" by Mark Kritzman of Windham Capital.[6] It goes to show just how much alpha a mutual fund or hedge fund needs to generate just to overcome their high fees and tax burden (quick summary: it's A LOT). Another good articles is

1 https://investor.vanguard.com/advice/personal-advisor
2 https://www.betterment.com/
3 https://www.wealthfront.com/
4 https://liftoff.advplatform.com/
5 http://assetbuilder.com/
6 http://assetbuilder.com/

John Bogle's "The Arithmetic of "All-In" Investment Expenses." [7]

We're not going to dwell on taxes too much, but we leave you with the simple advice to place all the assets you can in a tax-deferred account. Further, any taxable assets should be managed in the most tax-efficient way possible with tax-harvesting strategies. ETFS are often a superior tax vehicle over mutual funds or closed end funds due to their unique creation/redemption feature. The website ETF.com has a good education center[8] for those looking for more information on ETFS.

7 http://johncbogle.com/wordpress/wp-content/uploads/2010/04/FAJ-All-In-Investment-Expenses-Jan-Feb-2014.pdf
8 http://www.etf.com/etf-education-ce.html

CHAPTER 13

SUMMARY

I would classify both my mother and grandmother as traditional Southern cooks. Their style was very much of the "finger" variety. While they may have a broad recipe to go by, the food usually was sampled with many tastings and the adjusted to the individual's preferences, etc. I spent a lot of time as a child in the kitchen making chocolate chip cookies with both of them (also known as my chunky years). That style of cooking often reminds me of asset allocation and investing. As long as you have some flour, baking soda, sugar, eggs, butter, and chocolate chips—the exact amount really doesn't matter. Some people like vanilla in the recipe, other people nuts, and some even more chocolate. But as long as you have some of all of the main ingredients, the results are usually similar, and delicious. (I rarely made it to the final product as I was more of a cookie batter kid.)

Investing is similar. As long as you have some of the main ingredients—stocks, bonds, and real assets—the exact amount really doesn't matter all that much. Does adding small allocations to emerging bonds (nuts), frontier markets (vanilla), or more chocolate chips (stocks) vastly change the outcome? Not really. The only thing that does really alter the outcome is if you go and mess with all the ingredients while they are cooking—a sure recipe for disaster. The single biggest take away from this book is to not ruin your allocation by paying too much in fees.

Below is a quick summary of the findings from this book. Many of the steps below are similar to the same suggestions we provided in our first book, *The Ivy Portfolio*, back in 2009.

- Any asset by itself can experience catastrophic losses.
- Diversifying your portfolio by including uncorrelated assets is truly the only free lunch.
- 60/40 has been a decent benchmark, but due to current valuations, it is unlikely to deliver strong returns going forward.
- At a minimum, an investor should consider moving to a global 60/40 portfolio to reflect the global market capitalization, especially right now due to lower valuations in foreign markets.
- Consider including real assets such as commodities, real estate, and TIPS in your portfolio.
- While covered more extensively in our other three books and white papers, consider tilting the equity exposure to factors such as value and momentum. Trendfollowing approaches work great too.
- Once you have determined your asset allocation mix, or policy portfolio, stick with it.
- The exact percentage allocations don't matter than much.
- **Make sure to implement the portfolio with a focus on fees and taxes.**
- Consider using an asset allocation ETF, advisor, or other automated investment service in order to make it easier to stick to the portfolio and rebalancing schedule. Yearly (or even every few years) rebalancing is just fine. Even better, rebalance based on tax considerations.
- Go live your life and don't worry about your portfolio!

FAQS

Where can I find software or a website to backtest my own allocations and strategies?

We send out a basic Excel backtester to subscribers of The Idea Farm[1] that will let you test all of the allocations in this book. Data will soon be updated through 2014. Below are a few free or low-cost options you can access on the web:

- Portfolio Visualizer[2]
- Alpha Architect[3]
- ETF Replay[4]
- You can also download free data sources[5] to Excel and test on your own.

---

1 http://theideafarm.com/
2 www.portfoliovisualizer.com
3 http://tools.alphaarchitect.com/
4 http://www.etfreplay.com
5 http://mebfaber.com/2013/03/21/free-data-sources/

What about other asset classes?

This book is meant to describe the main asset classes that comprise the majority of the global market portfolio. The allocations provided in this piece form the basis for a core portfolio. However, many asset classes are perfectly reasonable in an asset allocation framework to include in the core or perhaps as satellite allocations— MLPs, infrastructure, emerging market bonds, municipal bonds, frontier market stocks, global TIPs, or even catastrophe bonds.

What about "Smart Beta" strategies?

Smart beta is a phrase that refers to strategies that move away from the broad market cap portfolio. (So in U.S. stocks, think the S&P 500 versus a portfolio sorted on dividends or perhaps equally weighted.) The market cap portfolio *is* the market, and the returns of the market portfolio are the returns the population of investors receive before fees, transaction costs, etc. However, market cap weighting is problematic.

Market cap weighted indexes have only one variable—size— which is largely determined by price. (While not the topic of this book, market cap indexes often overweight expensive markets and bubbles—you can find more information in our book *Global Value*.) Many smart beta strategies weight their holdings by factors that have long shown outperformance, including value, momentum, quality, carry, and volatility.

Here is a fun interview with William Bernstein[1] on factor tilts. We are big proponents of smart beta and factor tilts applied to a portfolio. Indeed, it is very difficult to beat a portfolio allocated one-third each to a) global equities with a value and momentum

1   http://www.etf.com/sections/features/19168-william-bernstein-be-open-to-new-factor-tilts.html

tilt, b) bonds, and c) managed futures or a similar trend strategy. We didn't want to dive too deep into smart beta strategies in this book since we have covered them so extensively in the past.

What about tactical approaches to asset allocation?

We firmly believe there are a number of strategies that work well in tactically managing a portfolio. Our 2007 paper, "A Quantitative Approach to Tactical Asset Allocation,"[2] lays out very simple momentum and trend-following strategies.

What about factors in sector or country rotation strategies?

There is evidence that these strategies can work as well. Our "Relative Strength Strategies for Investing"[3] paper outlines a very simple sector rotation methodology based on momentum and trends. Our Global Value[4] book looks at rotating countries based on value.

FIGURE 46 is a graph that looks at country stock rotation strategies based on various metrics. Note: You want the countries with the highest yield, worst trailing currency returns, and worst trailing GDP growth!!

Should I hedge foreign stocks?

We are actually agnostic on this topic, but once you decide on your choice to hedge or not, you should stick with it. Currencies go through periods of under and outperformance, but over time, real currency returns are very stable. The key words being over time.

2   http://papers.ssrn.com/sol3/papers.cfm?abstract_id=962461
3   http://papers.ssrn.com/sol3/papers.cfm?abstract_id=1585517
4   http://amzn.to/1h3pVfa

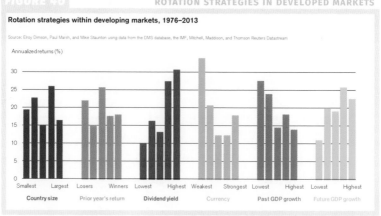

FIGURE 46

Rotation strategies within developing markets, 1976–2013

Source: Elroy Dimson, Paul Marsh, and Mike Staunton using data from the DMS database, the IMF, Mitchell, Maddison, and Thomson Reuters Datastream

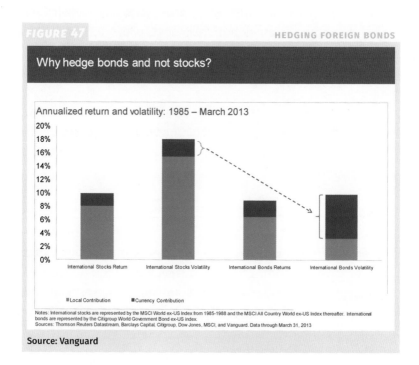

FIGURE 47

Why hedge bonds and not stocks?

Annualized return and volatility: 1985 – March 2013

■ Local Contribution   ■ Currency Contribution

Notes: International stocks are represented by the MSCI World ex-US Index from 1985-1988 and the MSCI All Country World ex-US Index thereafter. International bonds are represented by the Citigroup World Government Bond ex-US index.
Sources: Thomson Reuters Datastream, Barclays Capital, Citigroup, Dow Jones, MSCI, and Vanguard. Data through March 31, 2013

Source: Vanguard

Should I hedge foreign bonds?

Bonds are a little different. Since sovereign bonds in general have lower volatility than stocks, adding the additional volatility of currency returns doesn't make much sense and therefore hedging foreign sovereign bonds is reasonable. A good Vanguard paper on the topic is "Global Fixed Income: Considerations for U.S. Investors."[1]

How do stocks and bonds perform relative to various inflation regimes? And what about real interest rates?

Stocks and bonds perform best when inflation is below about 3%. Above 5% inflation and returns fall off a cliff.

The opposite goes for real interest rates, stocks and bonds love rates above 3%. While stocks hold up okay with lower real interest rates, bonds get clobbered.

---

1   http://www.vanguard.com/pdf/icrifi.pdf

FIGURE 48

Real bond and equity returns vs. inflation rates, 1900–2011

Source: Elroy Dimson, Paul Marsh, and Mike Staunton

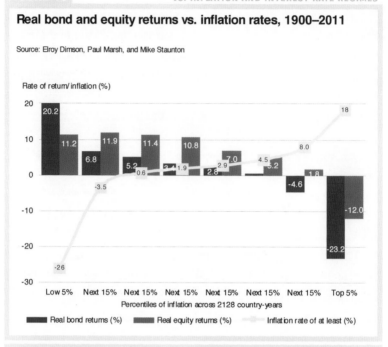

Real asset returns versus real interest rates, 1900–2012

Source: Elroy Dimson, Paul Marsh, and Mike Staunton, DMS database

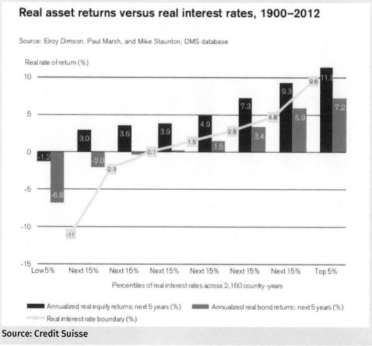

Source: Credit Suisse

THE TOBIAS PORTFOLIO

Andrew Tobias has written twelve books, including selling over a million copies of The Only Investment Guide You'll Ever Need.[1]

He proposes another basic Lazy Portfolio with only three holdings, which is also reminiscent of Bill Shultheis and Scott Burns's three-fund portfolios. The lack of real assets definitely hurt this portfolio in the 1970s.

---

1 http://amzn.to/1DbgZ6l

FIGURE 49

US Large Cap	Stocks	33%
US Small Cap	Stocks	
Foreign Developed	Stocks	33%
Foreign Emerging	Stocks	
Corporate Bonds	Stocks/Bonds	
T-Bills	Bonds	
10 Year Bonds	Bonds	33%
30 Year Bonds	Bonds	
10 Year Foreign Bonds	Bonds	
TIPS	Real Assets	
Commodities	Real Assets	
Gold	Real Assets	
REITs	Real Assets	

Source: The Only Investment Guide You'll Ever Need, 1978

FIGURE 50

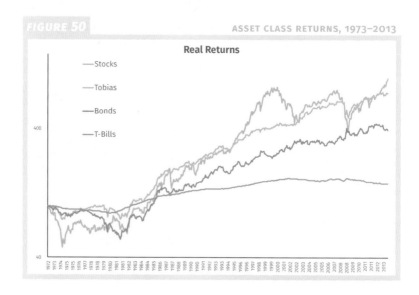

	T-BILLS	BONDS	STOCKS	TOBIAS
Returns	5.27%	7.74%	10.21%	9.66%
Volatility	0.97%	8.43%	15.57%	10.52%
Sharpe	0.00	0.29	0.32	0.42
Max Drawdown	0.00%	-15.79%	-50.95%	-35.73%

REAL RETURNS 1973-2013

	T-BILLS	BONDS	STOCKS	TOBIAS
Returns	0.99%	3.34%	5.71%	5.19%
Volatility	1.24%	8.73%	15.74%	10.77%
Sharpe	0.00	0.27	0.30	0.39
Max Drawdown	0.00%	-44.75%	-54.12%	-39.33%

REAL RETURNS 1973-1981

	T-BILLS	BONDS	STOCKS	TOBIAS
Returns	-0.71%	-5.08%	-3.92%	-2.95%

REAL RETURNS 1982-2013

	T-BILLS	BONDS	STOCKS	TOBIAS
Returns	1.48%	5.85%	8.61%	7.61%

REAL RETURNS 1973-2013

	T-BILLS	BONDS	STOCKS	TOBIAS
1970s	-1.55%	-4.23%	-5.26%	-3.27%
1980s	3.81%	7.22%	11.67%	12.38%
1990s	1.95%	4.87%	14.71%	8.24%
2000s	0.19%	3.92%	-3.38%	0.34%
2010s	-1.82%	2.17%	13.73%	7.91%
Volatility	2.38%	4.33%	9.78%	6.39%

Source: Global Financial Data

THE TALMUD PORTFOLIO

"Let every man divide his money into three parts, and invest a third in land, a third in business and a third let him keep by him in reserve."

— TALMUD

You can't get much more basic than this.

FIGURE 51   TALMUD PORTFOLIO

US Large Cap	Stocks	20%
US Small Cap	Stocks	
Foreign Developed	Stocks	9%
Foreign Emerging	Stocks	4%
Corporate Bonds	Stocks/Bonds	
T-Bills	Bonds	
10 Year Bonds	Bonds	33%
30 Year Bonds	Bonds	
10 Year Foreign Bonds	Bonds	
TIPS	Real Assets	
Commodities	Real Assets	
Gold	Real Assets	
REITs	Real Assets	33%

Source: Talmud, 500 C.E.

FIGURE 52   ASSET CLASS RETURNS, 1973–2013

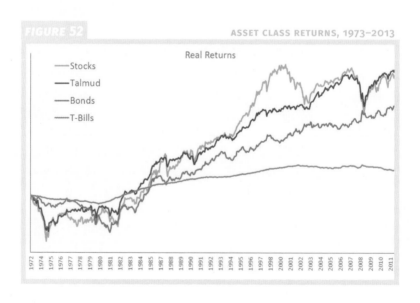

	T-BILLS	BONDS	STOCKS	TALMUD
Returns	5.27%	7.74%	10.21%	9.81%
Volatility	0.97%	8.43%	15.57%	10.46%
Sharpe	0.00	0.29	0.32	0.43
Max Drawdown	0.00%	-15.79%	-50.95%	-39.56%

REAL RETURNS 1973-2013

	T-BILLS	BONDS	STOCKS	TALMUD
Returns	0.99%	3.34%	5.71%	5.34%
Volatility	1.24%	8.73%	15.74%	10.70%
Sharpe	0.00	0.27	0.30	0.41
Max Drawdown	0.00%	-44.75%	-54.12%	-44.12%

REAL RETURNS 1973-1981

	T-BILLS	BONDS	STOCKS	TALMUD
Returns	-0.71%	-5.08%	-3.92%	-2.53%

REAL RETURNS 1982-2013

	T-BILLS	BONDS	STOCKS	TALMUD
Returns	1.48%	5.85%	8.61%	7.68%

REAL RETURNS 1973-2013

	T-BILLS	BONDS	STOCKS	TALMUD
1970s	-1.55%	-4.23%	-5.26%	-3.29%
1980s	3.81%	7.22%	11.67%	9.65%
1990s	1.95%	4.87%	14.71%	7.31%
2000s	0.19%	3.92%	-3.38%	4.10%
2010s	-1.82%	2.17%	13.73%	8.56%
Volatility	2.38%	4.33%	9.78%	5.22%

Source: Global Financial Data

THE 7TWELVE PORTFOLIO

The 7Twelve allocation was proposed by Craig Israelsen in 2008. Craig is the author of three books and is a principal at Target Dale Analytics.

7Twelve is one of the more consistent portfolios, having made positive real returns in every decade.

FIGURE 53

US Large Cap	Stocks	13%
US Small Cap	Stocks	13%
Foreign Developed	Stocks	8%
Foreign Emerging	Stocks	8%
Corporate Bonds	Stocks/Bonds	
T-Bills	Bonds	8%
10 Year Bonds	Bonds	8%
30 Year Bonds	Bonds	
10 Year Foreign Bonds	Bonds	8%
TIPS	Real Assets	8%
Commodities	Real Assets	17%
Gold	Real Assets	
REITs	Real Assets	8%

Source: 7Twelve Website, 2008

FIGURE 54

Real Returns

— Stocks
— 7Twelve
— Bonds
— T-Bills

	T-BILLS	BONDS	STOCKS	7TWELVE
Returns	5.27%	7.74%	10.21%	10.00%
Volatility	0.97%	8.43%	15.57%	9.20%
Sharpe	0.00	0.29	0.32	0.51
Max Drawdown	0.00%	-15.79%	-50.95%	-40.68%

REAL RETURNS 1973-2013

	T-BILLS	BONDS	STOCKS	7TWELVE
Returns	0.99%	3.34%	5.71%	5.54%
Volatility	1.24%	8.73%	15.74%	9.31%
Sharpe	0.00	0.27	0.30	0.49
Max Drawdown	0.00%	-44.75%	-54.12%	-39.76%

REAL RETURNS 1973-1981

	T-BILLS	BONDS	STOCKS	7TWELVE
Returns	-0.71%	-5.08%	-3.92%	0.59%

REAL RETURNS 1982-2013

	T-BILLS	BONDS	STOCKS	7TWELVE
Returns	1.48%	5.85%	8.61%	6.98%

REAL RETURNS 1973-2013

	T-BILLS	BONDS	STOCKS	7TWELVE
1970s	-1.55%	-4.23%	-5.26%	1.33%
1980s	3.81%	7.22%	11.67%	9.25%
1990s	1.95%	4.87%	14.71%	6.96%
2000s	0.19%	3.92%	-3.38%	3.58%
2010s	-1.82%	2.17%	13.73%	4.98%
Volatility	2.38%	4.33%	9.78%	3.05%

Source: Global Financial Data

THE WILLIAM BERNSTEIN PORTFOLIO

William Bernstein is a retired doctor based in Oregon and is well-known for his writing on asset allocation with at least 10 books as well as a blog[1] and investment advisory.

Below is his suggested allocation. Not surprisingly, with an allocation of 75% in stocks, the portfolio returns are very similar to the broad stock market.

---

[1] http://www.efficientfrontier.com/

FIGURE 55   WILLIAM BERNSTEIN PORTFOLIO

US Large Cap	Stocks	25%
US Small Cap	Stocks	25%
Foreign Developed	Stocks	25%
Foreign Emerging	Stocks	
Corporate Bonds	Stocks/Bonds	
T-Bills	Bonds	
10 Year Bonds	Bonds	25%
30 Year Bonds	Bonds	
10 Year Foreign Bonds	Bonds	
TIPS	Real Assets	
Commodities	Real Assets	
Gold	Real Assets	
REITs	Real Assets	

Source: The Intelligent Asset Allocator, 2000

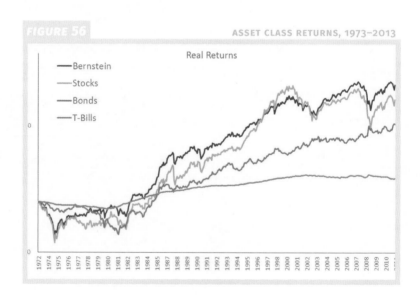

	T-BILLS	BONDS	STOCKS	BERNSTEIN
Returns	5.27%	7.74%	10.21%	10.34%
Volatility	0.97%	8.43%	15.57%	11.93%
Sharpe	0.00	0.29	0.32	0.42
Max Drawdown	0.00%	-15.79%	-50.95%	-39.50%

REAL RETURNS 1973-2013

	T-BILLS	BONDS	STOCKS	BERNSTEIN
Returns	0.99%	3.34%	5.71%	5.84%
Volatility	1.24%	8.73%	15.74%	12.16%
Sharpe	0.00	0.27	0.30	0.40
Max Drawdown	0.00%	-44.75%	-54.12%	-44.84%

REAL RETURNS 1973-1981

	T-BILLS	BONDS	STOCKS	BERNSTEIN
Returns	-0.71%	-5.08%	-3.92%	-1.67%

REAL RETURNS 1982-2013

	T-BILLS	BONDS	STOCKS	BERNSTEIN
Returns	1.48%	5.85%	8.61%	8.08%

REAL RETURNS 1973-2013

	T-BILLS	BONDS	STOCKS	BERNSTEIN
1970s	-1.55%	-4.23%	-5.26%	-2.27%
1980s	3.81%	7.22%	11.67%	12.40%
1990s	1.95%	4.87%	14.71%	9.38%
2000s	0.19%	3.92%	-3.38%	1.02%
2010s	-1.82%	2.17%	13.73%	8.09%
Volatility	2.38%	4.33%	9.78%	6.11%

Source: Global Financial Data

THE LARRY SWEDROE PORTFOLIO

Larry Swedroe is one of my favorite writers and researchers. With 15 books to his name, his focus on evidence based investing fits in well with how we view the world. We debated about including this portfolio in the book since it requires using a value tilt, but think it is an important example of how a simple smart beta strategy may be beneficial to the overall portfolio.

The biggest difference between the allocation and others in this book is that he allocates to small cap value. Small cap value stocks have outperformed broad small caps by about four percentage points a year, which is a lot. The value stocks have slightly more volatility and a higher drawdown as well.

Below are the portfolios returns for comparison.

Swedroe's unusual allocations are another example of a consistent performer due to including a mix of stocks, bonds, and real assets. We include the performance of including small cap as well as small cap value to illustrate the improvement in performance. The portfolio with the value tilt results in the highest Sharpe ratio of any portfolio in the book.

FIGURE 57   LARRY SWEDROE ELIMINATE FAT TAILS PORTFOLIO

US Large Cap	Stocks	
US Small Cap	Stocks	15%
Foreign Developed	Stocks	
Foreign Emerging	Stocks	15%
Corporate Bonds	Stocks/Bonds	
T-Bills	Bonds	35%
10 Year Bonds	Bonds	
30 Year Bonds	Bonds	35%
10 Year Foreign Bonds	Bonds	
TIPS	Real Assets	
Commodities	Real Assets	
Gold	Real Assets	
REITs	Real Assets	

Source: Swedroe

FIGURE 58   ASSET CLASS RETURNS, 1973–2013

	T-BILLS	BONDS	STOCKS	SWEDROE	SWED & VALUE
Returns	5.27%	7.74%	10.21%	8.63%	9.32%
Volatility	0.97%	8.43%	15.57%	6.04%	6.31%
Sharpe	0.00	0.29	0.32	0.56	0.64
Max Drawdown	0.00%	-15.79%	-50.95%	-20.61%	-22.79%

REAL RETURNS 1973-2013

	T-BILLS	BONDS	STOCKS	SWEDROE	SWED & VALUE
Returns	0.99%	3.34%	5.71%	4.22%	4.89%
Volatility	1.24%	8.73%	15.74%	6.19%	6.44%
Sharpe	0.00	0.27	0.30	0.52	0.60
Max Drawdown	0.00%	-44.75%	-54.12%	-20.99%	-23.99%

REAL RETURNS 1973-1981

	T-BILLS	BONDS	STOCKS	SWEDROE	SWED & VALUE
Returns	-0.71%	-5.08%	-3.92%	2.61%	-1.29%

REAL RETURNS 1982-2013

	T-BILLS	BONDS	STOCKS	SWEDROE	SWED & VALUE
Returns	1.48%	5.85%	8.61%	5.36%	6.40%

REAL RETURNS 1973-2013

	T-BILLS	BONDS	STOCKS	SWEDROE	SWED & VALUE
1970s	-1.55%	-4.23%	-5.26%	1.99%	-0.66%
1980s	3.81%	7.22%	11.67%	7.68%	9.26%
1990s	1.95%	4.87%	14.71%	5.09%	6.07%
2000s	0.19%	3.92%	-3.38%	3.41%	2.39%
2010s	-1.82%	2.17%	13.73%	4.54%	4.88%
Volatility	2.38%	4.33%	9.78%	2.11%	3.75%

Source: Global Financial Data

DISCLAIMER

The views expressed in this book are the personal views of the author only and do not necessarily reflect the views of the author's employer. The views expressed reflect the current views of author as of the date hereof and the author does not undertake to advise you of any changes in the views expressed herein. In addition, the views expressed do not necessarily reflect the opinions of any investment professional at the author's employer, and may not be reflected in the strategies and products that his employer offers. The author's employer may have positions (long or short) or engage in securities transactions that are not consistent with the information and views expressed in this presentation.

The author assumes no duty to, nor undertakes to update forward looking statements. No representation or warranty, express or implied, is made or given by or on behalf of the author, the author's employer or any other person as to the accuracy and completeness or fairness of the information contained in this presentation and no responsibility or liability is accepted for any such information. By accepting this book, the recipient acknowledges its understanding and acceptance of the foregoing statement.

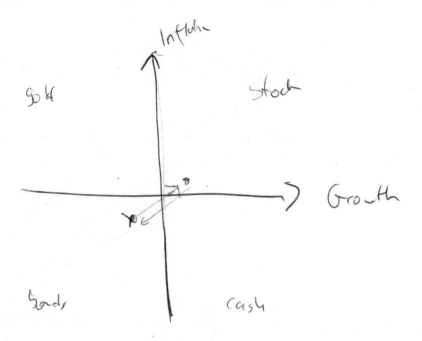

more info:
- market view
- high level what portfolio should be (quadrants)
- how do diff asset classes perform in diff environments.

Printed in Great Britain
by Amazon

17906891R00076